VISION

VISION

YOUR PATHWAY TO VICTORY

Sharing a Direction to a Better Future

GORDON
D'ANGELO

NEW YORK

VISION
YOUR PATHWAY TO VICTORY
Sharing a Direction to a Better Future

ISBN 978-1-61448-150-8 Paperback
ISBN 978-1-61448-151-5 eBook
Library of Congress Control Number: 2012935392

Morgan James Publishing
The Entrepreneurial Publisher
5 Penn Plaza, 23rd Floor,
New York City, New York 10001
(212) 655-5470 office • (516) 908-4496 fax
www.MorganJamesPublishing.com

Cover Design by:
Rachel Lopez
www.r2cdesign.com

Interior Design by:
Bonnie Bushman
bonnie@caboodlegraphics.com

In an effort to support local communities, raise awareness and funds, Morgan James Publishing donates a percentage of all book sales for the life of each book to Habitat for Humanity Peninsula and Greater Williamsburg.
Get involved today, visit
www.MorganJamesBuilds.com.

Habitat
for Humanity®
Peninsula and
Greater Williamsburg
Building Partner

DEDICATION

This book is dedicated to the thousands of believers who, through the relentless persistence of faith, align numerous varieties of energy to serve the good of all.

CONTENTS

Acknowledgments

The purity and power of this book is a testimony to God for the many gifts he has given his people. Therefore, I acknowledge and thank the original visionary and creator who is God. Just this one gift of vision is an example that He exceedingly provides the resources needed to obtain your biggest imagination.

Simplifying the process of this glorious power into words took nearly three years. Once the words hit the paper we were encouraged by the tangibility of this power. If not for dedication and persistence of my assistant and editor, Amanda Aksel, I would still be thinking about getting this work finished.

I would like to thank my first business mentor, William Birchmeier. Though he was extremely demanding in getting results, he taught me the purification process to capture the power of engaging individuals to obtain successful results. He taught perseverance, particularly in tough times, and led me and others to success amidst turbulence.

Some people provide inspiration and motivation perpetually. John Hewitt did this numerous times for many. He exhibited excessive results while encouraging all to participate in life's opportunities. He never gave up and would make any underdog feel encouraged and excited to move forward. Thanks to him my vision of life was expanded.

To the numerous Pastors I have known in my life; Pastor Williams and Pastor Tebbano, who dedicated their lives to helping and guiding others, while sacrificing the apparent riches of this world. They have nourished an incredible amount of happiness while the fruit of their unselfish efforts has flourished in the development of families, businesses, and thousands of people.

Let me express my thank you to NEXT Financial Group, Inc. for allowing me the time to write this book. They believe in openness, voice, and the ability to choose your own destiny. This culture has been fertile ground for the development of experiencing the freedom to create ideas and participate in projects at the highest level.

Chapter One

WHAT IS VISION?

WHAT IS VISION?

Everything starts with vision. Vision is the process that brings imagination to creation. Every function, everything that is, was created from something that wasn't there. The founder is visionary. You possess this power, and can use it as you wish. It is my vision that in one year you can take what you have learned from this book and make a positive and significant difference in your life and the lives of others. This book is a pathway for you to start authoring your vision and achieving your victory. You will learn many elements of vision and how you can author success in your own life. Remember, you did not fill out an application to be on this earth. You don't have to make installment payments, good days or bad; **life is a gift** and so is vision. This gift of vision is not an accident. It is a perpetual and dynamic resource for everyone to access. Much of this resource is utilizing the power of time. We are given a certain amount of time to enjoy and even struggle, but the experience of this existence we were given freely to create. Vision allows us the right and freedom to form the end-results that we choose to bring into existence.

Vision proves that all things are possible. Thousands of concepts that are common today were once considered utterly impossible, completely absurd, and unattainable. Imagine the laughter and mockery that you would have experienced 150 years ago if you discussed the idea of carrying multitudes of people across the globe in a metal shell with wings, traveling thousands of miles in only hours, or talking to someone from a great distance with a handheld wireless device. There are so many great discoveries and inventions that are not that impressive today, because we have learned to look beyond. Those are just glimpses of what vision is capable of achieving.

Clearly the successes that are going to exist tomorrow are not seen today, but someone's vision will bring them into play. **Why not yours?** Throughout this pathway, you will discover how you can apply this visionary process today. It is a guarantee that new visions will foster new creations, because you have been granted access to all the elements of the universe. The exponential combinations of these elements tied to energy have yet to be tapped. Uncountable, great things are in store as these combinations are tested. There is complete evidence that anything we get excited about today from microwaves, to computers, to cell phones, to jet planes were created by the tools that have existed all along. They were created by a combination of vision and time. Without vision, time would not have brought them into existence. By seeking the elements and energy in a visionary fashion, you are playing a much more confident and stronger position in the creations in your life. You can specifically create your desired intentions of the future by engaging in the visionary planning of today. The point is that the success you are going to have tomorrow is waiting for you to call upon its structure. Why not be clear and declare whatever more you wish for yourself. It's waiting for you to claim. That's the power of vision.

THE VISIONARY FORMULA

Einstein was considered a genius. Millions marveled at Einstein's ability to make complex astrophysical formulas short and simple. The most widely known example is $E=MC^2$. When astrophysicists and NASA do formulas with respect to rockets ships, the movement of asteroids, the development of solar systems, and the universe in general if E doesn't equal MC^2, it is generally believed to be incorrect. The **relativity** of this visionary process is simple. It is designed to help you follow visionary steps to achieve the end result. Deviating can cause your theory or approach to be incorrect. You will witness a visionary formula that we believe, will massively improve your visionary success. Those who take part in the process can advance themselves to a higher state of existence personally and professionally while having a positive effect on the lives of others.

Vision has a simple formula that can solve the complexities of your life and make it marvelous.

**Vision = the definable intention
from which preparation is formed.**

In other words, you have to begin with the end result. What is your definable intention? Then you make the preparation to get there. I will discuss this further as we move along the visionary pathway. First, I would like to go back to the beginning and tell you how I discovered vision, how I know it is the key to victory, and how everyone, including you, can achieve magnificent results with this God-given tool.

DISCOVERING VISION

When I was a teenager I started writing specific numerical results. No one told me to do it, and I didn't own any kind of business. It was just my nature to write down results. You may even call them goals. I wrote them for years to come. It was fun because I was free to enjoy the idea and relish in the possibility.

Later in life I experienced vision through other people, including my good friend John Hewitt. John was the instrumental force behind Jackson Hewitt and now Liberty Tax Service. One thing about John is that he believed anything was possible. I know because I experienced it. He believed that when he wanted to do something better, he could. He illuminated results long before the process. John was very magnetic in getting people to believe in what he was trying to accomplish. He was great at looking at things from different perspectives, including math. He could analyze a problem with different approaches and explain each successful end result. He was very good at explaining that the end results were attainable and connecting people to his vision. He was also very good at having people do what they are good at and utilizing their best talents. From a visionary perspective, I think his biggest asset was that he believed he could be the best at something and he was willing to put in the time. Nothing was unattainable to him. My experience with John was not only influential, but also inspiring.

When I began working for a national corporation, they required the following year's budget five months in advance. The common practice among my colleagues was to prepare a mild increase in growth and profit. So naturally I fell into the groove that single digit increases in growth and profit were acceptable, and therefore my objective. After my first year it dawned on me; *why can't I write a better future with a more aggressive budget, a bigger number, and then make the preparations?*

Being naïve and in my early 20's, I did not realize all the obstacles in the way of hitting double-digit increases. Most of my peers laughed. In fact, I felt they were pulling against me because I was rebelling against the commonality that modest increases were acceptable. Because I was following a formula, writing numbers was simple. Where was the obstacle? Who was holding my arm back? It was easy to write the numbers. To me, numbers were as visionary as they were when I was a young. It wasn't that I was better than everyone else. I believed in more potential in that what was not seen could come to pass. Since my numbers included definitive results, I then prepared and took aggressive actions to get to those specific results. Many of the things I did were new, and some of them failed. I improved the things that worked, discarded the things that didn't, but I constantly stirred the pot. Remarkably, year after year, I exceeded all of my peers' performance on an annual and cumulative basis simply because I wrote it first. The moral of the story is I would have never left the path of complacency and mediocrity unless I took the visionary pathway. This is something you can write and accomplish. Though I was naïve then, now I understand it was a combination of being fearless and knowing that what is yet to come, with vision, I could bring into creation. I decided to use this formula in the rest of my life.

The point is that vision can help you build something that otherwise would have never happened. Because of your vision, creation occurred. Everyone has many gems that they can bring to fruition if they just take a visionary approach. **Do you know what you could make appear? Do you have any idea the amazing power that you possess?** Making a significant change in your life whether it means generating more income, creating more long-term equity or gathering an army of allies is just a visionary plan away. It's my intention for you to master this process by using a really simple formula. Most people have all of those extra resources and gifts near them, and just don't know how to access and use them. The great news is that it is right next to you. You can choose to use the simple visionary formula and start being successful in your desires today!

Is a goal the same as a vision?

Goals are a component of vision. Sometimes they appear to be the same, but vision is the bigger picture. Goals tend to be personal objects in the short-term, and are not the wholeness of vision. They often do not include how succeeding promotes the success and gratification of others. A vision is made up of multiple items and categories of what you want in a three to five year period of time. Even if your vision is centered on you when it starts, as you move along the pathway it encompasses the betterment of others, and the creation of more visions.

SOCIETY IS NOT VISIONARY

Interestingly enough, we are all born visionaries but somehow, as we get older, we are immersed in a society that drifts us away from this victorious gift, and places us into being content with mediocrity. Society is not visionary. How many times did you hear, *you can't have that! We can't afford that! That is impossible! Stop dreaming!* What about the people who never hear those things? Don't they have a better chance simply because they expect it? By expecting it, they can author a vision that will deliver. The negative energy that emits from people telling you the reasons that you can't accomplish a certain feat will gradually build into a barrier. That can discourage even the most capable of people. It is clear that people who don't hear *"you can't"* **simply believe they are bigger favorites to win**.

Society has encouraged you into a pattern to find a job, buy a house, work 40 hours a week, and save for your retirement. Yes, many of those are great and honorable pathways and I'm not saying they are bad. They are regimented, structured, and in a sense, anti-visionary. Someone who says they want to work four days a week is considered radical. Why? Because there is a system in place that says five days a week is the norm. Having the idea to work four days a week instead of five is visionary because you created it and did not just walk into it. The next time you look at what society is dealing and you don't like it, you may be surprised to find that your own pathway can be easily achieved. The reason society is regimented is because it cannot deal with everyone's potential vision. It has to create structure. In many cases it makes perfect sense, like traffic patterns. For life in general, it seems that society creates a pathway to mediocrity in case you don't have an alternative plan. When you inspire vision you can surpass society's pathway and master its energy resources, avoiding the traffic and arriving there faster.

For example, it is expected that most Americans will retire in poverty. There is not enough money in social security and many people lack sufficient savings. So even relying on what appears to be stable sources for revenue could be an error. The stronger source to rely on is your own visionary pathway. The future you want, the future you shared and the future you created for yourself. It is no surprise that the greatest successes have come from those who have dared to be visionary. These are the people books are written about, and why can't we write about you?

For some people, vision may be a hard concept to grasp because they don't understand its simplicity. You may be one of them. People fear they have to be a genius and see things that others don't. The truth is that it is a very simple process. For example, we can't explain electricity completely. Yet, 300 years ago electrons were here. They have been here since day one. Electrons are really what generate electricity. Look at all the power you get from exciting the electrons. They were always here, but it wasn't until Ben Franklin and Thomas Edison that there started to be practical uses. Are we not made of electrons? Isn't that what we are? Sure.

Vision is the outlet. It is waiting for your plug. The energy is there, waiting to function as you direct. When you plug in the television, the television works. If you plug in a lamp, you have light. When you plug in your vision, it will function just as you envision. Our outlet is capable of entertaining any vision. If it doesn't you are saying the powers that be, are too small for your vision. I have yet to see that happen.

LINCOLN MEETS THE CELL PHONE

What other types of power are there that we don't understand? How many things have we seen manifested in our lifetime that did not exist before; cell phones, computers, Internet etc. If you were to go back in time and explain a cell phone to Abraham Lincoln, do you think he would understand it? Your conversation might go like this…

You

Hey Abe, this is a cell phone.

Abe

What's a cell phone?

You

Well it's something that deals with frequency.

Abe

What's frequency?

You

Well, it goes to a satellite.

Abe

What's a satellite?

You try to make it simpler by saying…

You

You can talk to somebody somewhere else.

Now he thinks you're demonic.

Now let's say you already had this conversation with Ulysses S. Grant. You turn the cell phone on and call Ulysses. Then you say to Abe Lincoln, "Ulysses is on the other line." And he takes the cell phone and says, "I don't believe it's him. Who's in here? What evil is this?"

Then Ulysses rides up on his horse and Abe is on his horse, and they look at each other talking through this device and Abe says, "Wow, that's amazing! I just have one question for you. How many minutes does this come with?" Just kidding!

They couldn't understand it. They couldn't believe it, but now they know it works even if they don't know how. You can understand how people from the 1850's would be astounded by the inventions of today. The same holds true for people of the 1950's.

Interestingly enough, when I speak to people of the 21st century and discuss the simplicity of vision, they look at me like Abe might have looked at you, completely perplexed. Yet, Abe Lincoln would have loved to have a cell phone, and would have said, *Show me how to use this. Show me how to help people.* Are you one of those people who will say *Show me how to use vision. Show me how to help people?* Be honest.

VISION IS A HIGHWAY AND A DESTINATION

The majority of people seek short-term comfort and instant gratification. Vision will provide a more complete and constant gratification with long-term comfort. It is designed to create and that creation helps others in numerous ways that the visionary had never considered. Simply put, there is another level waiting to be discovered, and from there others. Mathematically there are more elements and combinations of power available than current human intelligence can harness.

Vision is a destination that identifies exactly where you want to go, what results you want, and when. You need to be specific. Many people have a general idea of where they want to go. Such as: *I want to be successful, I want to have a career, I want to get married, and I want to buy a house.* The vagueness of these destinations and the immensity of what you could have versus what you're thinking you could have is a huge difference, and will have a massive effect on your life. Whether you are perceived as a huge success or content to be a successful person by your own standards, you still need to have a vision that clearly illustrates the destination. Clarity is a substantial part of vision. Many people have imagination, desires, hopes, dreams, goals and they call them visions, but they are not complete. They are just the tingling of inspiration for you to write a vision. They are reminders of how close you are to the power. If you stop at the tingling, you won't get the full sensation of the immensity of visionary success and gratification, which in truth never ends. Here is confirmation.

Now to Him who is able to do exceeding abundantly above all that we ask or think, according to the power that works in us. (Ephesians 3:20)

This Bible verse proves that His power is available in you to accomplish anything.

Most accomplished visionaries will admit even though they were the spark that created the vision and the driver at the wheel, they are quick to acknowledge that the energy they drew near them was exponentially far more than what they could ever imagine. Visionaries can't imagine it, because it is an unimaginable amount. It's hard to explain unimaginable amounts to people, but there are more stars in the universe than there are grains of sand. That's very hard to think about. It would take a person multiple lifetimes to write the numbers of zeros in miles that exist in the universe, because the distances in space are so vast. Your role is to have the vision. Don't worry about the other energies and resources that will fuel your vision, just **be the spark!**

Watching your vision evolve is an embryonic process that continues to expand and accelerate far more than you and others can handle, if you choose to take it there. If you can have unimaginable results, how easy would it be to obtain imaginable results? In this embryonic process, in a very short period of time, you will start to see the entrance of energy and other resources come to the aid of your vision. Just like the outlet that is waiting for you to plug into, the amount of energy you could attract can be significantly more than what you can imagine. It happens by the definable intention we call vision.

VISION RECEIVES RECOGNITION

Vision receives recognition, and becomes an attraction for others. Writing a vision and sharing it with others will create a following. People will remember, respect, and elevate you because of your vision. Wow! Have you been waiting for that? It is not even the accomplishment of the vision, but the possession of the vision. When I told people I would be writing this book and have it finished by the end of the year, many said, "Great, send me a copy. I can't wait to read it." As time moved on, they would ask me how my book was progressing. I would respond, "What do you think and feel about vision?" I would get their comments. By sharing it, there is an attraction of energy and others. You can get their comments and count the energy. It is a tangible source that amasses near you. What is great about this small act is it holds you accountable for your vision. You set out to do it and believe it or not, people want you to succeed. Even though you haven't finished the work to get you to that stage of accomplishment, you're recognized for identifying the accomplishments that you want. Just like a student whose says, "I'm going to school to get my PhD in business and then work for a company as a junior executive. After that I will start my own company and run a new operation in a different state." Wow, they haven't done it yet, but he is getting recognition for the fact that his vision is demonstrable to other people and that's very important. Vision gives you more credibility. Because of that credibility, you'll get more recognition and respect when people are relating to you. Your credibility is higher because you have a vision that has been shared. It also opens the door for the energy needed to support the end result. You will be surprised to find out how many people really want you to succeed. Initially, in a subliminal way, you have made them an energetic part of this process.

I tell you all these things because it is important that you understand what vision is and how it can help you achieve things that you thought were never possible. More than that, it works! I want you to understand that vision and Strategic Visionary Planning is simple. I will show you how unparalleled success is right around the corner as we continue the pathway to discover your vision and achieve your victory.

Chapter Two

THE VISIONARY PROCESS

STRATEGIC VISIONARY PLANNING

The way to get started is to use a process that I call Strategic Visionary Planning. Strategic Visionary Planning (SVP) became a technical term used to harness the energy, great ideas, aspirations, and personal talent to a higher level. The key behind SVP is that you, the individual, author it and agree completely with your conclusions. You can apply it to your personal life, professional life, business or any specific category.

When I introduce Strategic Visionary Planning to someone it brings them tremendous comfort. There is great acceptance of SVP because it is an inviting and refreshing reminder of the power of your life. It is a healing process to get your life more focused in the direction of your choice, and to follow through on the destiny you were meant to have. Understand that the input is your creation. SVP is a power that simplifies your complex thoughts and desires into a powerful short list. It's a prophetic equation about you and your future.

THE VISIONARY TEMPLATE

Strategic Visionary Planning starts with the visionary template. This template is a pure and easy-to-use tool. It is a freely-open platform to list the specific things you would like to bring into creation. It is simply a list of what you want, and when you want it. It's almost childish in the sense that it is so pure. It allows you to give yourself a brain check and ask, *is this really what I want?* That is as simple as I can make it.

In my experience, regardless of the simplicity, 99% of people don't have anything similar or written in a transferable form. They don't realize how this can harness the power of their lives. It makes great sense that productive, intelligent, and driven people have a simple format to gather the energy of others. If you do nothing else, be sure to complete your template and share it. This is the strongest part of SVP!

Your vision is simply what you want. Think about the results you seek in your professional and personal life. Think like a child for a moment. Believe that **all things are possible**. What is it that you really want? Take a few minutes to write them in the space provided on page 21.

Visionary Template

December 31, 2020

1.
2.
3.
4.
5.
6.
7.
8.
9.
10.

AUTHORING YOUR VISION

It's great if you know your vision by heart and in your head, but it is significantly more important that you write it down. I cannot stress this enough. There is a biblical verse that illuminates this very principle.

The Lord answered me, and said, Write the vision and make it plain upon tables that he may run who readth it. (Habakkuk 2:2)

Your vision can get started on a piece of paper, a sticky note or even a napkin. I have tons of initial visionary numbers written on napkins. It doesn't matter what you write it on as long as you start by writing it down. With this process, you will turn your vision into a flier that can be shared with other energy sources. Keep your vision with you. This is going to be a big part of sharing and building your connection chain, which we will talk about more as we move along.

You can achieve your vision simply by authoring it, sharing it and using the visionary formula.

**Vision = the definable intention
from which preparation is formed.**

ANATOMY OF A TEMPLATE

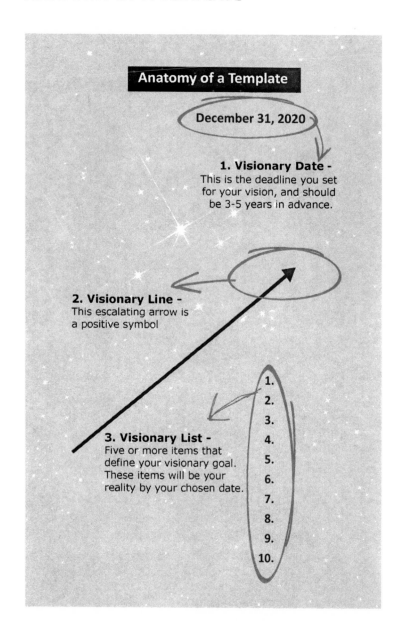

My Wish List
example

1. Work less

2. Spend more time with my family

3. Make more money

4. Increase my business profit and equity

5. More one on one time with clients

6. Better quality of clients

7. Help others

8.

9.

10.

My Wish List

1. _____
2. _____
3. _____
4. _____
5. _____
6. _____
7. _____
8. _____
9. _____
10. _____
11. _____
12. _____
13. _____
14. _____
15. _____

The most important part of the formula is "definable intention". Your vision needs three things to be ultimately defined. These are very important pieces and should not be left out. Just as players on stage, each has a role that makes the entire show a success. Let's make the movie of your life an Academy Award winner! A well-defined vision is measurable and tangible with a timeline.

SVP should begin with a timeline. Your target date should be no sooner than three years. Somewhere between three and five years is ideal, and usually year-end or December 31st of your chosen year. The reason for a three to five year timeline is because you don't want to wait significant periods of time to see if results are coming to pass.

For example, you want to deliver canned goods to the food bank. In regards to vision, you don't want to declare that you just want to deliver canned goods to the food bank. How many canned goods or how much weight do you want to deliver? This is the measure. When do you want them delivered by? This is the timeline. Give it a number. Numeric statements are an easy way to demonstrate measurability. A vision has to have precise numbers because numbers are not vague. 15-20 is a range, but 20 is exact. How about two tons of canned goods to the food bank by the end of the year? These definitive points are necessary to engage more sources of energy to the specific result.

Measurability is important because you need to be able to track your progress. In the meantime you can measure how close you have come. By the middle of the year, you may have delivered a ton of canned goods to the food bank. Now, you know how far you have come and how far you have to go. Measurability marries the definable intention to the timeline. The time you give yourself to achieve a vision is vital to its efficiency, realization, and inspiration to all contributors.

Tangible means that you can touch it. If you said, "I want to be more inspired" or "I want to be happy", those are great things, but they are not tangible. They can be, but you have to apply measurability to it, making what seems intangible, visible. If you say, "I want to deliver two tons of cans to the food bank" that is tangible.

> ***What if my vision is to be happy? Isn't that just as much a part of vision as things that are tangible?***
>
> *Yes, being happy can be visionary. How can you measure happiness? Maybe you want to measure happiness by smiling 20 times a day every day, or making 10 positive statements about yourself every day. Having a vision aimed at happiness, love, satisfaction or contentment is great! It is visionary. Happiness and love in my opinion do not have boundaries. So whatever level you are at you can always go to a higher level if you choose.*
>
> *For Example:*
>
> *One woman wrote on her visionary template that she wanted to spend one week with each of her daughters who were grown and lived in different states. I told her that her vision was more than that and I asked her again. She said that it was to bond with each of her daughters. So I suggested that she call*

each of her daughters and tell them that she wanted to bond with them and that they could all come up with one idea that would help them bond while she was visiting. Here we defined intangible intention, gathered the power of others, and illuminated its measurability and vision. Not only did the daughters come up with multiple ideas, the daughters got into a competitive mode on which one was going to bond more with their Mom. Before she even went to spend the week with each of them, they were all increasing their bond. The bonding started to occur because she brought the vision into creation. She identified the tangibility. The tangibility originally was not clear, but because she shared the vision, it came to light and it came to pass. Others were helping her instead of her putting in the love and effort alone. That is an example of the power of vision.

THE VISIONARY PROCESS

Visionary planners are directors of ample power, excessively beyond your imagination. Successful access is easier when you have systemic approach. Strategic Visionary Planning brings tremendous personal value to the growth of your wealth and a fuller experience of your life. The reason it is adding value is because you are playing a bigger role rather than just being there. I have seen many people become wealthy and they are not happy, because it only added financial value and not personal value to their lives. The visionary process is simple, and by following these steps you will change your life and the lives of others.

The first step only takes about 15 minutes to initiate. Start by picking your visionary timeline. By what date do you want to achieve your vision? Now you can begin to author your vision by listing what you feel is most important. Make your visionary list of items, but list at least five items of the measurable and tangible place you want by your chosen timeline.

Be careful to not list activities. Those will come into the process later. You might say I want to buy my first house. Then you define it by saying it has to have 3500 square feet, four bedrooms, and two and a half baths. None of those are activities. They are quantifiable measures.

For example a businessman may start with this:

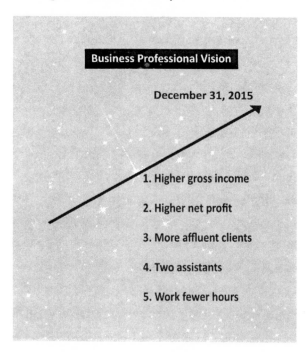

In this vision, the author has listed five items that he would like to see in five years. He knows that he wants to make more money, work fewer hours, have better clients and more help. Many of us think in these general terms and wonder why we are not getting the results that we want. You want a higher gross income? How much gross income? You want more affluent clients? What defines affluence? Give it a number. You want two assistants? What results do you want from your assistants? You want to work fewer hours? How many hours do you want to work and when do you want to work them? Clarity magnifies your vision!

It is okay to start off weaker and get stronger. Vision involves consistent improvements. Edits are allowed. Every one of these items can be broken down in more definable terms. When you get to the root of what you really want and write it down in tangible and measurable terms you have significantly increased the power of your vision coming to creation.

On the next page is an example of a more defined vision from the author.

Now we see the transformation. This author has illustrated his definable intention. Just by writing it down, he has created a tool that will help him focus his energy and his efforts on the things he wants to bring into fruition. The first vision could have been brought to fruition, but because it was not defined he would be wondering why the vision came to be and why he is still not satisfied. The old saying is *"be careful what you wish for."* In this scenario, *"What you write will come to light."*

Part of the visionary process is the act of sharing your vision. That is why it is so important to write it down and be clear. Clarity and simplicity make it easy to understand. The people you share

Business Professional Vision–Revised

December 31, 2015

1. Gross income of $500,000

2. Net profit of $380,000

3. 60 Clients with a net worth of $1,000,000

4. 2 Full-time licensed assistants

5. 30 Hour work week

your vision with, whether in your professional industry or personal life, should understand what is written. You have to think, *if I was handing this to others what would they say? Would they understand it?* You also want to think of it backwards. If someone gave you this vision, what would you think? What would you tell them? Even if it is not your line of work, would you still understand it? When you have a well-defined vision, others will understand and connect to it. They should be able to repeat it, and even claim part of your vision as theirs. This is when you witness the enlistment of others energy.

In my experience, everyone is encouraged by SVP. It is a peek into their own future, in which they have a controlling interest and a controlling role. So they love it. It may take two, three or four times before it is definable and measurable. In coaching SVP, measurability, timeline, and definition rule. You are the one who makes the decision that what you are writing is what you want.

My vision is in my head. Do I have to write it down?

There was a man who had a vision, but it wasn't illustrated. His vision was in his mind and even in discussing it at a dinner party or with friends it would change a little bit. No one took it that seriously because it was just commentary.

He would say, "Oh yeah, Sally and I are looking to buy a new house." And, "I'm looking for a better job. I need to make more money." It was vague and nobody caught onto it. There was a disconnect.

Then there was another person who did Strategic Visionary Planning and put what was in his head in the visionary template. His vision was very specific, and he used it as a tool to focus his energy. He wanted a new job in a particular field with a specified salary, and a new house in a located area with definable criteria. He began to share his newly written vision with everyone. People not only understood that he was focused, but several had suggestions to bring him closer to his vision. One of his connections got him in touch with a real estate agent that specialized in the area he was looking. Another connection got him in touch with someone who worked at a company with jobs in the field that he desired.

Now what's the difference? The first vision was in his mind and considered common. It had no connection or calling for energy. In the second case it became illustrative of a result and that started to attract resources, which makes all the difference in the world!

A DEFINABLE INTENTION

The more definable your vision the easier it will be to bring the result into existence. The definition and measurability create a pathway that starts to amass energy immediately, heading directly toward your visionary points. Someone who has three visionary points for three years up the road on their list, that's good. Someone who has five visionary points, that's better. Someone who has five visionary points with sub points under each of them is best because it is a more definitive illustration of the content.

When you define the blue print like an architect, you don't go off the pathway and start breaking down walls, rebuilding walls in the middle of your vision, go on rabbit trails, or lose your focus. That's why this template is so important. Everything should be incredibly clear.

For example, one person I did visionary planning with said that he wanted to hire two financial advisors. I thought, just *any two advisors?* I didn't understand what that meant because you can hire any two advisors today! What is the measurability? Do they have to have any production? Do they have experience? Do they have a client base already? In doing this process it starts to reverse the way you think. Think about the end results first, and then you can fill in the blanks.

FAITH LIKE A CHILD

When it comes to vision, thinking like a child is a good place to start. Have little fear, be completely unaware of obstacles, and have faith while you anticipate many things happening in your favor.

If a child is asking for a birthday gift what do they do? They tell their mom or their dad. *I want a red toy truck for my birthday.* That is visionary. They want a red toy truck and they want it by their birthday. Nowhere along the line does the child ask what their parents taxable income is, how much disposable currency they have, how far the mall is, or even if it is in stock. The child expects their request (vision) in a timely fashion, because they shared their vision with the only resource that they know. *That is having faith like a child.* They are too young to realize that doubt is an enemy. Children don't perceive obstacles, or create obstacles

Business Professional Vision–Final Revision

December 31, 2015

1. Gross income of $500,000

2. Net profit of $380,000

3. 60 Clients with a net worth of $1,000,000

4. 2 Full-time licensed assistants
   a. Manage 200 new client processing
   b. Retention Rate 98%

5. 30 Hour work week

in what they want. They keep it simple. They expect they will get this toy by this date simply because they are asking for it. Imagine that the same child writes their request in a note to their mom and dad. It is the same request, but it becomes more powerful. The parents are impressed by the note and unbeknownst to the child, share it with other people. Mom and Dad are introducing the child's vision to another resource, and guess what? Those people the parents share with are attracted by this energy, and those people want to get that gift for that child or be involved in some way. What an amazing example of having a vision and sharing it!

You are trying to make something come to be by writing your vision and while you are writing it you are thinking *How?* **Stop!** It's time to be wise and have faith like a child. If you worry and judge yourself, you become an obstacle to your own dreams. Why should you be an obstacle to your dreams? To keep it simple, write the vision and don't doubt it. Expect it. You can say it is your fantasy vision or whatever you want to call it, but if you write it and share it, it's a real vision. That vision is going to happen. The likelihood of it happening will increase even more as you train your mind to be visionary.

Why is the format important?

The format is important because most of us look for a guide or a system. This format is simple and ignitable! Having this template allows you to sort out those thoughts into a clear and defined vision. It's like having the seeds in your mind, and having a place to plant them. The template makes it simple, measurable, and saves you time; it's easy to share and it lets you know when you are going on a rabbit trail.

Think of a weight scale. You weigh less this week than you did last week. It's simple and easy to understand. It can be measured. Vision is the same way. Are you closer or farther away? It is easy to make excuses and lack discipline. Your only asset is time. How do you want to use your time? If you want to use it to aim it towards your vision then you need a format. If you want to use your time to rabbit trail like crazy, you can. There is no instantaneous penalty for that except what you could have been is now delayed. The format protects you from yourself and constant interference.

Hebrews 11:3 reads, "things which are seen were not made of things which do appear." Everything that exists comes from something we once couldn't see. If you want it to come to pass your words need a place to become alive. This template is one such place. Even if it seems like it isn't perfect or in the right format, just getting started is such a positive lift from where you are and where you are going to end up. You start to put distance between you and the ordinary. It may be the most important thing you ever do.

When you write down your vision you will start to feel the sense of your power. You will witness the connection to your own authored vision. You will see energy attracting to the very essence of what you have written. It's good that you don't have the answers of how. It's okay at this point because it takes the inhibitions away. Now instead of being on tracks going nowhere, this track is going to a specific station that you have chosen to exist. You will put yourself in an elite company with the fact that you can initiate creation.

There is a biblical passage that I like to share when I talk about vision.

Where there is no vision, the people perish. (Proverbs 29:18)

The reason I share this is because I want you to understand the importance of your vision. This passage doesn't necessarily refer directly to you perishing. If you have no vision others may perish; people you don't know, and people you may never meet. It's concerning that you don't know whom else you are affecting by not being visionary. Henry Ford invented the first automobile assembly line, which revolutionized the mass productions of automobiles. He didn't know that it would evolve to change the entire economy, and how the world does business. The auto industry has created millions of jobs around the world all because Henry Ford dared to be visionary. Without his vision others would perish. With vision the people shall flourish.

THE CONSTANT VISIONARY =
THE CONSTANT VICTORY!

Being visionary dramatically increases the positive experiences in your life. Though visionaries seek more adventure they are constantly being fulfilled and gratified. If you've ever said, *what is it I am missing*, you will get a taste of the answer when you start Strategic Visionary Planning. You begin to realize and acknowledge your potential openly, while inspiring other's growth and infinite part of this new expansion you have ignited.

Can I modify my vision?

Yes, you can change your vision. Yet try to keep its DNA. Changing your timeline is major, but changing the essence of what you want is more severe. If you are going through a life change then maybe it is the right move. This is why agreeing with your visionary plan is so important.

You have to be sure to stop yourself from going on rabbit trails or at least reduce the amount of activities that are not related to your visionary results. The visionary template is an alarm that indicates if your activities are tied to your definable intention. **If you can't identify the connection to your vision, it is a rabbit trail! Ding Ding!** *Be sure to check your alarm because there are so many seemingly-related opportunities that in fact are distractions, and can pull you away from your focus. The temporary accomplishment may seem worthwhile, but if it is not tied to your vision then you have redirected your energy and lost efficiency.*

Stay on your course. Vision is your pathway to victory!

Now that you understand more about the visionary process, it is your turn to author your vision. Take a look back at the wish list you filled in on page 21 . Take the same ideals, be a child, be

Your Visionary Template

Date:_____

Name:_____

1.
2.
3.
4.
5.
6.
7.
8.
9.
10.

_____

pure, and write your vision. Go ahead! This visionary template is a blank canvas waiting for your requests to be brought to life.

When you have completed your template you can go back and spend another 15 minutes with it the next day to check and make sure it is in the necessary format.

REMEMBER IT NEEDS TO BE

- Definable
- Measurable (numeric)
- Tangible
- Describe results, not activities

It is better to do this now for a few minutes of your time, than to go on rabbit trails which cost you years of your time. By doing this process it puts you miles ahead of where you were before. It makes you a promising contender in the race. This makes you a player and separates you from the commonality of normal busy people who don't reach the finish line as fast as you.

BRIDGE NUMBERS

Bridge Numbers are your vision dissected by year. It is a way to show the progression of the results, and inspire others to help your vision happen. A five year vision will have five bridge numbers.

It is easier to measure and report numerical needs and successes. Both which can be used for improvement, and prescribed systemic energy. You don't want to wait five years to find that your vision is not coming to pass. You can break down your definable intention on an annual basis, a quarterly basis, or a result that you want at your next meeting.

Just like the universe, everything works backwards. First there is creation, then reality. The visionary template is the same. First there is the visionary template, then your reality. The important thing to note about bridge numbers is that they expand and accelerate. This means that every category will grow and improve with time. The increase of your result should be bigger between year four to five than year one to two. In other words, your biggest acceleration takes place at the end. Think of it like college. Are you smarter in your first year or your fourth year? You are better, faster, and smarter as time goes by, and that is how visionary bridge numbers work.

For example, if you are trying to improve 120 units over a five-year period. The common mistake is to improve 24 units a year over five years.

This is incorrect, because it shows that there is slower growth. If you go from 24 to 48 it is 100% growth. If you go from 48 to 72 it is only a 50% growth. (See page 42).

Expansion and acceleration are part of vision. It is the evidence that your vision is coming to pass. Your bridge numbers should expand and accelerate, particularly more toward the end.

Now you can break down your vision annually. Use the template on page 44 and give it a try!

AGREE AND SIGN

After you complete the revisions of your visionary template and your bridge number template, review it one last time. Take in the possibilities of your vision and really visualize it in your mind. Are you excited? Does it feel right? If the answer is no, it's okay. Come back the next day and do another revision.

Remember it may take a few tries before it is most defined. If you are excited, and it feels right then you are ready to get started. Before you move on to the next step in Strategic Visionary Planning, make a commitment to your vision and sign it. Put your John Hancock right on your vision symbolizing the agreement you have made with yourself to stay focused and persistent along the pathway to your victory!

When you focus your energy on your defined vision the power increases and continues to increase daily and perpetually. It starts to do its gravitational magic on your neural-pathways, which makes your mind more active and powerful. That power multiplies daily because you are going to be on a higher level on day two than you were on day one, better on day 30 than on day five and so forth. SVP is a lot like taking dance lessons. Every time you do a step or maneuver you move up a level. There are more levels, it's more exciting, and you feel that growth and sense of accomplishment. The visionary planning intensifies, but the effort lessens. The strain and stress reduce, but your level of perception of the future increases. You are enjoying it more, and your gratification permeates your mind and body. You are now seeing existence clearer, like focusing in on a telescope. If you look at a foreign substance or pictures of the universe, the more times you do it the more you recognize it. In vision, the things that you are seeing and recognizing are things that you put there. There is one object the first time you look. The next time there are two or three items, and the next time there are four. Strategic Visionary Planning is not a finite status. It is endless. You can't catch up to all the things you can create, but wow, it's a great ride!

Bridge Numbers

2011

1. Gross income of $90,000

2. Net profit of $60,000

3. 10 Clients with a net worth of $1,000,000

4. No assistants

5. 40 Hour work week

2012

1. Gross income of $150,000

2. Net profit of $90,000

3. 15 Clients with a net worth of $1,000,000

4. 1 Part-time licensed assistants

   a. Manage 25 new clients

   b. 80% Client Retention

5. 38 Hour work week

2013

1. Gross income of $200,000

2. Net profit of $100,000

3. 20 Clients with a net worth of $1,000,000

4. 1 Full-time licensed assistants

   a. Manage 40 new clients

   b. 85% Client Retention

5. 38 Hour work week

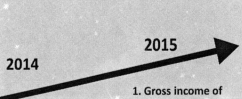

2014

2015

1. Gross income of
   $275,000

2. Net profit of $190,000

3. 30 Clients with a net
   worth of $1,000,000

4. 1 Full-time licensed
   assistants
   a. Manage 100
      new clients
   b. 91% Client Retention

5. 35 Hour work week

1. Gross income of
   $500,000

2. Net profit of $380,000

3. 60 Clients with a net
   worth of $1,000,000

4. 2 Full-time licensed
   assistants
   a. Manage 200
      new clients
   b. 98% Client Retention

5. 30 Hour work week

Year 3

Year 2

Year 1

44 Units

28 Units

14 Units

Year 3

Year 2

Year 1

72 Units

48 Units

24 Units

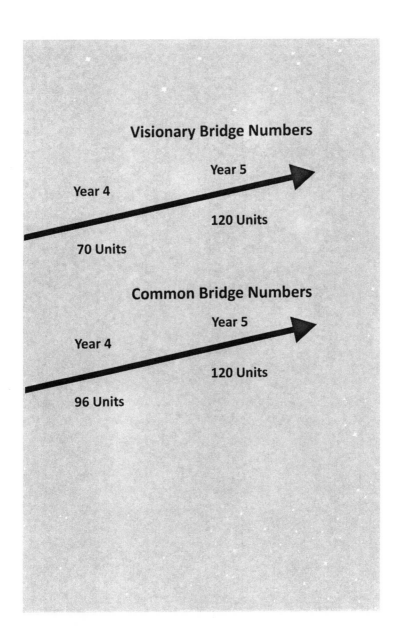

Visionary Bridge Numbers

Year 5

Year 4

120 Units

70 Units

Common Bridge Numbers

Year 5

Year 4

120 Units

96 Units

Bridge Numbers

Year 3

Year 2

Year 1

Year 1

1.
2.
3.
4.
5.
6.
7.
8.
9.
10.

Year 2

1.
2.
3.
4.
5.
6.
7.
8.
9.
10.

Year 3

1.
2.
3.
4.
5.
6.
7.
8.
9.
10.

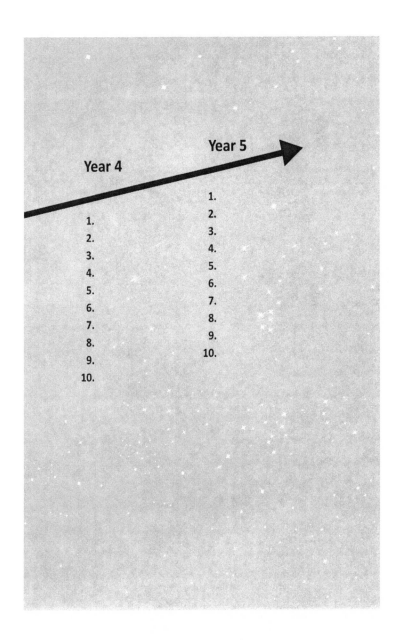

Year 4

1.
2.
3.
4.
5.
6.
7.
8.
9.
10.

Year 5

1.
2.
3.
4.
5.
6.
7.
8.
9.
10.

Eventually you will become your own coach and you will coach others with regard to Strategic Visionary Planning. When you willingly apply this effort you will overcome. You will do better for your family and yourself. You will realize you are the highly active ingredient inspiring the outcome of many futures.

Chapter Three

INITIATIVES

WHAT ARE INITIATIVES?

Initiatives are the next step in Strategic Visionary Planning, and should be started after you define your vision. When you authored your vision and bridge numbers, I bet many of you were asking *how* all of your vision is possible. Writing your vision is a special place where obstacles don't exist. Now the vision needs initiative to spark them into reality. Vision comes first, initiatives wait. This separates the genius from the worker bee. Initiatives are the creative preparations or productions that are designed to create identifiable percentages of the vision. The more focused initiatives are the better your army, and the bigger chance it has to produce 100% of the vision. One initiative might produce 7% of the vision. Another might produce 15%. Each initiative should have a responsibility to its fractional relativity to the vision. The point is that you have to create initiatives with a definable result in order to produce the complete vision. Initiatives without identifiable results in a specified timeline are rabbit trails, which we will discuss more as we move along the pathway.

Every stage of the visionary process starts with a definable intention. Initiatives must do the same. Your initiative might be to have a conference call. You can have conference calls every day. What is the result of having that conference call? Is it to get 50 more users to a product, increase your client base by 5%, or build a business relationship that you intend to bring to another stage? Whatever the case, you want to identify the definable intentions before the call. The call is the initiative, but it still has to go through the visionary process. The more specific you are the better. At the end of the call you have to ask yourself (and your teammates) if the call produced the results that you defined.

Initiatives are the activity. There should be lots of verbs when you do your initiatives, but it doesn't escape the fact that it has to be tied to a result. Remember, activity does not win the day. Activity helps the day. Results win the day. Many armies have been very busy and very active and yet, they have lost the war. Directing activities towards results will greatly increase the ability to obtain those results.

For example: Your vision is to generate 10,000 new clients by 2020. You can start with 20 initiatives, which average 500 new clients each. That's visionary. You don't need to know what the initiatives are at first.

Pick a number of initiatives that is higher than what you think you can come up with. I usually use 80 because it pushes me to get creative and think of innovated ways and seek ideas from other people. You don't have to define the initiatives to start. You simply have to identify the number of initiatives and the result they will produce. Later, this will become a valuable nucleus to attract powerful energy and resources. Initiatives are laid out much like bridge numbers, though they do not correspond with bridge numbers directly. However, the results should be based on and equal to your bridge numbers for each year. If your bridge number for the first year is to get 400 new clients then create your initiatives to reach that bench mark. Here is a breakdown using the example of getting 10,000 new clients with 20 initiatives.

Each year you are increasing the amount of initiatives and therefore yielding an increased result.

Intuitively we start with the idea of just one initiative, but what happens is the false hope that the one initiative is the *be all end all*. It never happens that way. One sure thing about initiatives that you must realize is that initiatives have to evolve. An initiative that is successful now may not be as efficient later. Whether it is outdated or tired, its longevity as originally designed is limited. When a child goes to school it is with the intention to graduate with an education after 12 years. When the child is in school does he just do one activity, take just one class? No, the child does many activities that create a well-rounded education, which expands and improves over time. Initiatives are the same. The level and performance of initiatives rise as they mature. This is a compounding, fun process which separates the distance between your greatness and commonality.

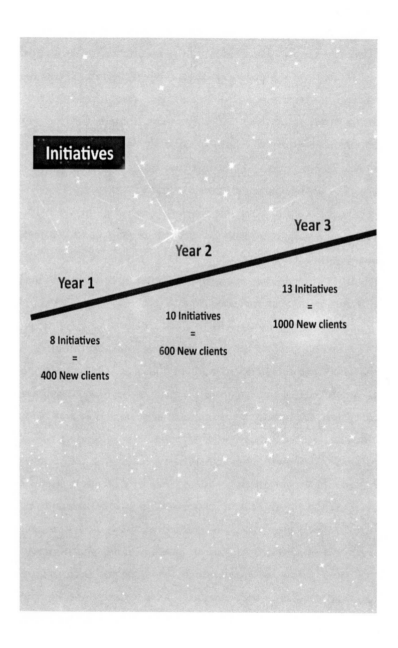

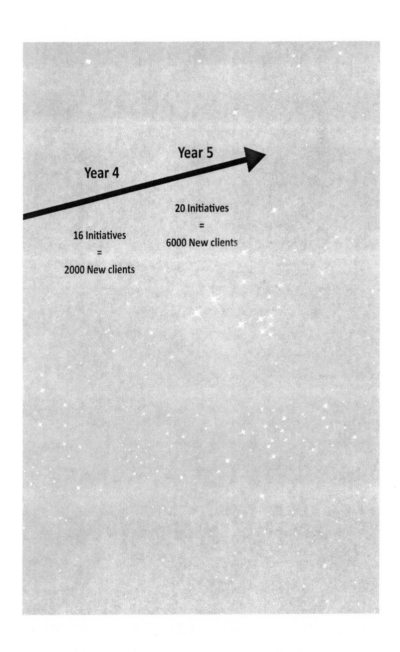

Year 5

Year 4

20 Initiatives

=

6000 New clients

16 Initiatives

=

2000 New clients

Most people don't have enough initiatives. They have over-exaggerated confidence in one initiative. They reach the contentment level of the process too early, and consequently they reach a false peak. Initiatives inspire growth on a perpetual basis. You can tell by the visionary footprints of expansion and acceleration, meaning that your initiatives are constantly reaching out farther at an accelerated pace and dominance because you are perfecting their growth.

Here are the five points of initiatives
1. **Create new initiatives**
2. **Measure the initiative to the intended result**
3. **Discard initiatives that are not working**
4. **Improve initiatives that are working**
5. **Repeat the process**

You will find that your initiatives are not necessarily unique to start. The difference is you are applying the defined result ahead of time, and stirring your creativity as defined by the five points. Designing initiatives is another process that you can share and receive input. You have to be careful not to get stuck in the trap of just one initiative. You have to constantly improve, discard and invent initiatives in order to keep the pipelines going. Initiatives are meant to expand. It is okay to start with small initiatives. Think of a tree that starts out as six inches tall. Eventually it will be 50 feet tall. Do you chop it down because it is six inches tall? No, because it is at the beginning stage. If you are going to keep it that small then it's not really a tree. If you confine your tree it's not going to grow.

You have to continually give it light from everywhere, which means others input and partial ownership. The key is to keep the tree growing. By letting your initiatives branch out in girth and strength you will get the results you need to succeed.

THE LION'S SHARE

Winning is fun. It's a party! Hitting visionary results is a recognizable achievement that will help so many. You will make yourself a unique commodity in your community or industry. If your initiative is to hold a cocktail party to sell 100 units and get 20 referrals that will make appointments in the next 30 days that is a defined intention for that cocktail party. When you go on to your next initiative, for example, a luncheon and then a movie event, by the time your competition tries to replicate your initial initiative, you're already doing the sixth or seventh initiative. Secondly, while they are doing phase one for the first time, you have done that initiative five or six times. You have already mastered the initiative to a higher degree. So if I go to their cocktail party versus your cocktail party I'm going to say, "This is far below par of what I am used to." Your competition is not designing initiatives based on definable results and your evolved efforts will get the lion's share.

INVENTING INITIATIVES

This can be extremely fun in addition to being beneficial. To start, define the number of initiatives you want to invent. This creates the expansion of your mind, and the ability to capture ideas that exist and the ingredients to create new ideas. Invite people to give you ideas: employ, delegate, and ask for help. Talk to people who are doing or have done the general concepts of your vision.

There are hundreds of people locally and nationally who have succeeded in growing their business, building a connection chain, and increasing their profits. Though their businesses may be different, the processes they have used for success may be very enlightening. You may not think so, but these successful people are very willing to share. Just ask! You have access to these winners, and it will give you pages of new ideas and new connections. I am certain there are hundreds that would be willing to talk to you. It's also good to get input from the people who are going to receive your product or service. Talk to clients or customers and ask them what they look for in a product or service. It's good to have their perspective to formulate new ideas. The interesting part is that you will have more ideas in a shorter period of time than you could have come up with by yourself.

Initiatives have to be persistently perpetuated. Once you stop creating and improving initiatives, you significantly slow your vision. You fall back to the others that you were surpassing. Many companies become complacent because they become successful. They stop improving and adding initiatives. Some companies change too much, and they forget some of the basics that got them to where they are today. You have to find the balance, and it always has to be reviewed. The flow of success starts with one initiative. Pretty soon you will have two initiatives, three, and then four. They can all be terrible, but if you are improving some, discarding some and adding new ones then you are on the right course that will lead you to success.

Here is proof. Can you make a hamburger? Yes. If so, can you sell billions like McDonalds? McDonalds started out as a local business in California in the 1930s, and is now the biggest fast-food hamburger chain in the world. Why? They are constantly improving a simple concept. They expanded into other fast food products; French fries, milkshakes, coffee, McThis, and McThat. It is the process that won, not the product. Execution has to be delivered, but improvements have to be constantly pursued. Many times, it is the process of taking an old idea to a new level. McDonalds' idea is to feed people quickly and efficiently. That's an old idea. Think of all the ways McDonalds improved: having a drive-thru, breakfast service, later hours, and faster service. The idea didn't change, but the process improved. Most of the inventing is in the process, not the final product. It's the perception and delivery that makes the world-class difference.

Eventually in this process, you come up with the right combination. Keep in mind that even the right combination can get stagnate down the road. So continue with the five points of initiatives. The question is where are you content? Do you want a little drip, double drip or do you want the flow? If you want that flow to get to your vision more efficiently then you have to be consistent. There is no limit to what you can do if you strive to find what works.

EFFICIENCIES

You already have initiatives with definable intentions and timelines. To understand efficiency you have to determine if these initiatives have delivered the predetermined results in the scheduled timeline. If it didn't occur, you have to toss it away. Eliminating a non-productive initiative early is efficient. How do you know when to eliminate an initiative? You measure your results against your visionary timeline. If that initiative does not yield those results then it certainly is not efficient. You need to decide if it can be improved or discarded. Make the decision quickly and move forward from there. It is that simple. Many people wait months or years and spend thousands if not tens of thousands of dollars on activities and initiatives that are a huge distraction. When you do away with time losers, you are doing a positive and proficient thing. Of course, if it is efficient and generates 50%, 70% or even 100% of your definable intention you still need to be attentive to the process by improving its efficiency to avoid slowing down the acceleration and expansion of your vision.

The entire visionary process is constantly being used. Having a visionary template is efficient. Sharing it in a finite fashion, improving, and integrating all the points that we have discussed is efficient. Efficient, productive, improvement seeking visionaries leave their competition behind while developing a very recognizable entity.

WIN THE DAY

You win the day by producing efficient results from a series of initiatives that accomplish your visionary intentions.

Is there a rule of thumb to decide if an initiative should be discarded or just needs improvement?

You decide. Yes, you have to give new initiatives time. Older initiatives should meet a certain criteria, but they are always under constant editing and measurement. When a network has to decide whether or not to dump a TV show or put a new one in its place, they look at the numbers. If, in a few months, it's not great then you should change it, and if it's getting better then you keep the initiative and continue improving.

Remember, adding and improving initiatives is the key to meeting your visionary timeline. You will find that as you fine-tune initiatives you can begin to delegate. Initiatives should always go to, what I call, **the delegation of initiatives,** *meaning you are able to replicate massive results, get extra quantities, higher levels of credibility, and you don't have to be the one doing it. There can be other people, groups or teams, clusters of energy working on your behalf. Now how efficient is that? Remember that vision expands and accelerates. Ultimately, mastering this process leads to the final stage in visionary planning which is to replace yourself. Soon you will have other people creating, improving, and discarding initiatives and you are elevated to a higher level.*

THE D.A.D. PRINCIPLE

The D.A.D. principle is an extension of the visionary template like bridge numbers and initiatives. The acronym stands for Definable Intention, Accountability, and Due Dates. Every initiative that you create needs D.A.D. Often like a Dad, D.A.D. keeps you and the initiative on track. Let's say you start a new marketing initiative that involves direct mailing. Now you apply the D.A.D. principle. Do you just want to send out a mailing or do you want a result from the mailing? First, of course, is to define your intention. What is the intention for the mailing? Is it to increase sales by 40%? Get 10 new clients? Sell 1,000 more units? Once you know what the intention is you have to name who is accountable for the result. Is it you, someone on your team, or the team itself? Who needs to follow through on the initiative and gather the results? Accountability also means who is in charge of improving, or discarding that initiative. List the names of those accountable. When you define what it is you want, and who is handling it you need to have a due date. What date do you want to complete your intended results? Is your due date in one month, six months, or two years? If you follow the D.A.D. principle you will surely keep your initiatives on track.

INITIATIVE D.A.D. EXAMPLE

<u>Create Mailing</u>

Definable Intention

Mail 500 post cards

Get 10 new appointments

Gain 5 new clients

Accountability

Mailing– Betty Assistant

Appointments– Bill Associate

Gain Clients– Brenda Associate

Due Date

Mailing– June 1st

Appointments– July 1st

Gain Clients– August 1st

COMMITTEE SUPPORT, PANELS AND PRESENTERS

Sharing and connecting others to your vision is one of the most important aspects of SVP. Whether it is an employee, a friend, a resource, or what is called a starter, when their spirit gets involved they become and remain attached. A prominent way to do that is by sharing the vision and letting them have voice and power. Continue to share data with them. One of the best ways to do this is to set up a committee or panel to illuminate their value, which creates further adhesion of their energy to your vision. We started numerous committees and have received brilliant ideas from those players. Some of them are not paid, but in all cases their voice and contributions are being recognized connecting them to a psychological gravitational pull.

Every person is, in some form, an energy force for your vision. Sharing and asking for input regularly is an easy starting point. Most often every one of these sources contains more power than you can imagine. Inspiring this energy requires repetitive action. Approach them with positive feelings, and show accrued results. Thank them for their participation in the vision, acknowledge their contributions, and allow them to lead you to other energy sources. It's always positive when your vision is integrated into their energy field.

ILLUMINATE YOUR PLAYERS

List the people you know or know of that can contribute to your vision. Whether they contribute ideas, capital, access to more resources, knowledge or just encouragement, you can illuminate and connect them while expanding and accelerating the visionary process.

Key Players List
example

1. *Mary- Marketing Professional*

2. *James- Customer Service Specialist*

3. *Bob- Products Adviser*

4. *Jack- Banker*

5. *Anna- Support Staff*

Key Players List

1. _____
2. _____
3. _____
4. _____
5. _____
6. _____
7. _____
8. _____
9. _____
10. _____
11. _____
12. _____
13. _____
14. _____
15. _____

EXPONENTIAL EXPANSION

When I was young, my teacher gave us a project in math class. The project was to take a 5x6 checkerboard, which had 30 spots, and double the number of every box. I started with box one and doubled the number so that box two was two, box three was four, box four was eight, and by the time I got to the 30th box the number was over half a billion. At first appearance it doesn't seem that continually doubling the 30 squares would add to such a high number. Expansion and acceleration use the same logic. It does not appear that building your illuminated players and connection chain will increase to uncountable numbers, but now you see the logic is simple.

This exponential expansion is what happens when you go through all of the stages of planning. Some areas will expand faster than others, because of where you are in life, the nature of your initiatives, and to whom you are delegating. If you create new visionaries, they're going to have initiatives and delegating, and results will follow. How many of those can you create, five, six, ten, maybe 30? If you've created ten, then aren't those ten going through the same stages and creating one, two, or five more? Soon you are getting cubed results of your original creation, which can be multiplied by a higher power. It doesn't take that many visionary creations to get to millions or even billions, though it does take a little time. The interesting thing is that the new visionaries are not the same. They are going to do something different. Will they do something less effective? Yes. Will they do something foolish? Probably, but they will also manufacture some new major effective points. Your leadership requires you to stay focused on your vision publicly and to communicate and share so that these improvements can get you to your definable intention. While this process continues it gets bigger and better, and that is part of the exponential expansion.

INTEGRATION

Integration means maximizing the valuation and flow of all the energy that you are creating. It is a massive improvement of efficiency. Most of the values, whether profit or equity, are already there. Learning to capture these categorical values through integration means that you will also capture a bigger slice of the future.

To picture this, imagine you put your hand in your pocket and you have some quarters. You put your hand in your other pocket and you have some smaller change. Then you put your hand in your back pocket and there are single and five-dollar bills. In your last pocket, you find hundred dollar bills. Most people do not have their hands in all of the pockets that they are controlling. They are used to settling for having their hand in any pocket.

Integration is a form of a pipeline. In a company that sells pizza, pizza sales are the valuation. However, if the company decides to have a brand name like The Pizza Box then the name can have value based on the success of the pizza. They can also take the pizza, freeze it, and sell it in grocery stores. The company can also decide to make their own cheese, grow their own tomatoes, and manufacture their own boxes. They are taking it to the next level by creating this pipeline of value.

Most companies don't realize the equity and profit that exists. That is improved by efficiency. It is also improved by increasing the awareness of all your team to look out for ways to capture the equity and profit. Needless to say, most businesses should be in the expansion mode and consequently capture more of the business that is in the field.

Let's say your company makes envelopes and you know you have to ship them in a box, why not manufacture and sell the boxes too? It applies to almost every form of business around. I am not saying to be massively multi-dimensional, but I am saying that there are direct correlations to increase your profit and equity. The more you integrate, the more you are guaranteeing a bigger margin of result. Integration is simply another avenue to connect others with your vision.

DEFINING ENERGY RESULTS

In every stage of vision you must start with the definable intention. In order to gather energy you have to start bringing people into the picture. If I am integrating 10 people into my energy field I will start by identifying what I want from each of them. Perhaps I want four new leads, four ideas, and two opinions. I am trying to get them to actively comment and subsequently they become connected and committed to my vision. I am not sure which comments are coming from which person, but I do know that I have identified that I want four leads, four ideas and two opinions. If I am not getting that then I have not integrated properly. You have to define it as an important project, identify the end result, and let them know you need their expertise to play a role in taking the journey. Make it enjoyable for them. Without their expertise, you will not make it there as safely, strongly and as powerfully. Now you have given them respect and illuminated their input. You have stimulated their activity toward the vision even if it is not the end result. It is still stirring the pot, but now with a definable intention.

INVESTING YOUR TIME AND USING THE VISIONARY PROCESS

If you were to invest $100,000 over the next four years, wouldn't you expect to get a return on your investment at the end of the four years? If you didn't get a return on your investment wouldn't you be upset and want your $100,000 back? What if you couldn't get your $100,000 back? Would you be furious?

Now ask yourself, what is more important, your time or your money? The answer is clearly your time. When you run out of time it doesn't matter how much money you have. If your time is so important, after four years don't you want to get the investment on your time and what you wanted for your time? So if four years go by and you don't have what you wanted, then something went wrong or you have inappropriately invested your time. Then yes, you should be furious. You can always get the money back, but you can never get your time back. The reason we inappropriately invest our time is because we don't have a vision. Vision magnifies the investment of your time, the result, gratification, and the numerous fulfilling points that the element of time possesses. You have won the day; you have extracted creation from your time, and made your existence worthwhile.

Chapter Four

SHARING
YOUR VISION

SHARING YOUR VISION

This part of the process is imperative to the accomplishment of your vision. Many think that if they understand their vision and they have the know-how that is all it takes. Almost always, this comes up short. The truth is that when you don't share your vision you are limiting its potential and boxing it in. If you want to finish somewhere in the middle or end of the pack, keep doing it this way. However, if you want to win, follow the truth, and share your vision. Sharing your vision is the second most important step after writing it down. That is why the visionary template is so important, because now it is easier to share. It is there to be shared. The point of writing it in definable, measurable, simple terms is so that anyone can understand your vision; even if they are not part of your industry or business. You can always tell the people who share their vision, because they are lively and enthusiastic.

Enthusiasm comes from the Greek word Entheos, which means the spirit of God within. Sharing is more spirit oriented and can magnify the spirit to new heights and new dimensions. You know that your sharing is right if the person can repeat it to others, sometimes using the exact definable terms. Like the phrase, imitation is the sincerest form of flattery, it is confirmation that your vision is extending to other energy sources. People transfer that energy. That is ultimately what you want.

Sharing brings things out into the open. It lets others know your intention. There is an unlimited amount of energy you can capture, and it starts with sharing. One of the things that restrain energy is a guarded mentality. Discrimination is another. When you don't share you are subliminally saying that this form of energy cannot help me; but in fact, the seemingly weakest strand of energy is often stronger than you. Why would you pass on a strand of energy that could give you access to all the resources you require? Some people who share their vision and passions are selective. They are prejudice. *I'll share it with my spouse. I'll share it with my co-workers. I'll share it with some friends.* The truth is the more people you share it with the better. There is no reason to play your vision close to the vest. What do you have to fear; more assistance, more power? Energy seeks other energy like a magnet. To truly be a part of it, it has to fuse together. Sharing your vision is like exercise. If you do it consistently, your vision will be in better shape, have more strength, and lasting longevity.

Many times corporations tend to be discriminating. Though they are focused on vision, they are often lax on gathering the very team of energy that they are employing. In addition to that, companies neglect to share within their own company by limiting the vision to its own department. It is completely the wrong attitude. They don't have to be directly involved, but can become indirect beacons of energy. If nothing else, clearly, they can feel included.

Often employers think they are sharing because they are telling the employees what the vision is and renting their behavior alone. It can be very rigid and disconnecting. Unfortunately this creates a lot of inefficiencies, which is what they were trying to avoid by limiting what their employees did. When you share, you allow your vision to be heard and their input to be heard. Others are then willing to promote, nourish, and grow the idea simply because you made them part of the end result. In every successful corporation, you will find someone at the top that is extremely passionate. They conveyed that passion down to their employees for the sake of a singular vision; meanwhile allowing the team to create subsequent visions. Visionaries inspire others to be visionary. Being part of something creates a stronger energy force. If you can create a strong energy force of unlimited, numerous people that can be a part of your vision, then why would you limit it to two people or 200 people?

CREATION OF A MAGNETIC FORCE

Vision creates a magnetic force. This magnetism increases by the amount of passion that you have, and by the amount of time you spend sharing your vision with others, connecting them to the end result. You will start to see proof in the number of people that are performing to assist with your vision. Sharing your vision has an exponential growth factor, because each of them may be presenting or expressing your vision to others that they know. People that you have never met or will never meet are now somewhat connected to your vision. Any of these touches could be the difference maker and game changer.

When you start sharing your vision, you are creating a new strand of DNA. We don't know all the parts of the human DNA. All we know is that the human strand is being created, which is a complex genetic composition that constantly seeks to improve itself, and so will your vision. It is not completed overnight, but it does begin to work evidently in your sight. Each person that you share with has a place, because they understand what the DNA wants to be. That is the definable intention you shared.

Two things happen when you are creating this energy and center of influence. First, gravity is occurring and pulling what your vision needs into its field force. Second, it protects you from extraneous deviations that will steer you away. Quickly you can identify what is in your atmosphere. You are not only creating a magnetic force, but a protective field.

If you are passionate and communicate your vision enough, others will ultimately come across your magnetic field and be drawn to inquire. You become an attraction for people who want to connect to that vision. Some people want to connect to your vision for their own purposes or self-made desires. Others will connect because, unknowingly, they need a place to connect. It's fun and something that benefits their lifeline. The key is that it becomes an energy source that has a pulling effect, which has constant attraction. It's not a onetime deal. I believe, individually, we can be confined energy with limited geographical communication. Sharing opens up the universe of geography and communication.

You can make it as big as you want. The bigger your sphere of sharing, the more elements will be attracted and start to perfect their energy toward your vision. Larger elements, forces, and people, who can have larger and quicker effects on the outcome, will get caught up in the magnetic force of your vision. The magnetic field you create takes a little time. However, it is always expanding and accelerating because it is gathering the energy to serve its purpose. Improving a new form of energy is a combination of hundreds of positive forces. If it is just you, your magnetic field will be limited, while the amount of force you can create by sharing is unlimited.

PHIL THE JANITOR

I've told this story many times. It is a reconstruction of a similar event that demonstrates the miracle of sharing your vision.

There's a teacher. She works in an orphanage where they need to hire volunteer teachers to work. One afternoon she is writing on a hallway chalk board. It reads, *Wanted- 6 volunteer teachers by September 1st.* The teacher sees Phil in the hallway. What is Phil doing there? He's the janitor. He's sweeping the floor, doing his normal duties, thinking about light bulbs that need to be changed and other jobs to do that day. So she goes over to Phil and says, "Look at the board. We need six volunteer teachers by September 1st."

Phil is thinking to himself, *Leave me the heck alone. I'm the janitor, what do I have to do with this?* So a couple of days go by, and the teacher sees Phil again. Phil is sweeping, minding his own business, and thinking, *oh here she comes again.* She says to him, "Hey Phil! We got a teacher. We only need five more!" She changes the number on the board. Phil is thinking again, *Okay, I'm sweeping, where's the light bulb.* He's just doing his job, right?

Three more days go by, she gets one more teacher. She says, "Phil, we got one more we only need four." Phil is just absorbing at this time as he sees the number on the board change again. Then the next time she says, "Phil we got three. We only need three more!" Phil is beginning to feel the energy, which is replacing his complacency. Now a week goes by. The teacher walks down the hall and sees Phil again. This time Phil looks up at her and says, "How are we doing on those teachers?" What a turnaround!

Do you see what is happening? The teacher brought him into her vision. She connected him, just like you can connect people to your vision. Do you think Phil is praying for her and thinking about getting more teachers? You don't know, but obviously he cares.

Later that month, Phil is working his weekend job at the museum. What does he do at the museum? He is a janitor. So one afternoon he is sweeping, and the museum curator walks by and asks, "Phil, how are things at the orphanage?"

Phil replies, "Great! We needed six volunteer teachers, and now we only need two by September 1st."

The curator smiles and says, "It just so happens that my sister Phyllis just moved here from Cincinnati, and she is looking for something to get involved with. Phyllis is very resourceful, and I know she would love to help."

Can you see the power? The teacher doesn't know whom Phil knows. Now that's just one person, Phil the Janitor. I picked the janitor distinctly in this story, because in our minds we picture Phil as a low intellectual resource. Phil is a great example because he is easy to overlook. Why should I share anything with Phil? The question I have is, why not? The fact of the matter is you can't tell me what kind of resource Phil is. He is a resource. In the story, how much energy was spent? The teacher walked down that hall, she shared it with him, and only occasionally. Did she give him money? Did she spend hours with him? No, she connected him, because she shared her vision. She made him part of it, and that small act helped move her vision forward.

The moral of the story I am trying to illustrate is that the teacher was willing to share her vision with everybody, including someone who seemingly could never help. She walks down the hallway sees someone else and shares it with her and sees someone else and shares it with him. With her time, passion, and sharing the vision grew. The teacher may not be a superstar, but she certainly was a sharing star, because she understood how this process increased the power of her vision.

If you want to simplify the whole process of visionary creation the two things to do are; write it and share it. That's it! The vision is the seed and sharing plants the seed.

Is visionary magnetism the same as the law of attraction?

The law of attraction means like attracts like. In other words, you attract what you are dispensing. Visionary magnetism is a more definable source in which fulfillment can be obtained. When we think about fulfillments from a psychological, emotional or eating perspective, much of the fulfillment is short term. Spiritual fulfillment is all the time. Visionary magnetism creates that kind of fulfillment. You are feeling fulfilled a lot more during your day, which is an attraction. It's true that through sharing and creating your magnetic field, you will begin to attract the provisions and people that are instrumental to the achievement of your vision. However, these accomplishments have much more to do with sharing outwardly than just holding on to your inward thinking.

A MENTAL SEAT TO YOUR GAME

A great example of a magnetic force is sports teams. People from Ohio will say, "Cleveland is my team!" Sorry to disappoint you folks, but it's not their team. First, the fans don't pay their bills or the players' salaries. They couldn't afford to pay for the team. They don't profit financially from the team's revenue. Secondly, the players on the team are not from Cleveland. They are from all over the country and they change seasonally. So why are the fans proclaiming it is their team?

People will pay large amounts of money for tickets to go and be part of that event. Fans are pulling for things. They want to touch things. They want home runs, baskets, and touchdowns. They want points to be scored for their home team. That is what the fans are screaming for. That is what they want. They know the big game is next week. The fans are not playing in the game, they are not paying for the game, they are not profiting from the game, but they are part of it. Why? Because the team has their name on it, their city's name on it, and they feel connected to it. If the team loses, then the fans moan and groan. When the team wins, fans are often ecstatic and exhilarated. It affects their life. They have spent energy on something to which they were connected. Energy is driven there. The manager of that team controls the chemistry of the players. If the team wins, he affects the lives of people who gravitated to that team, people who he is never going to meet. The team manager is thinking about his job and his results. He's not thinking about affecting the lives of people in the city. That's not in his job description, but he will affect them; because they gravitated and connected to that team.

Sports are very simple. The team with the most points wins. What are the standings at the end of the season? This is very tangible and measurable with a time line. Make your vision the same. Think in terms of a season, standings, and measurability. You have to break them off because you do not want to have lifetime standings. You need to refresh and restart. Why does it have to work that way? Because it connects people. If they said your home team is going to play another team, and there are no standings, no winning for playoffs, no measurability, accountability, it would lessen the ability to share and connect. It doesn't lessen who wins, but tracking makes it easier to claim their connection.

During the first Super Bowl, Kansas City versus Green Bay, there were so few people in attendance. They had to move the people to the middle of the field so the cameras could see them, and the stadium appeared to be packed. Now, Super Bowl tickets sell for $2500 to $20,000 per seat, if you can even get one. That was something created by the National Football League, a group of people who took a sport and connected millions of people before there was cable. We all have that same power.

The point I'm trying to make is the things that connect people are things we can create in advance of the story. Every person has this ability. In a way, people have the ability to create their own football league and their own Super Bowl by explaining their criteria, measurability, time line, and creating this gravitational force that will grow, enhance, and develop perpetually. With vision, you can create your own home team. When you share your vision, believe it or not, people are mentally buying tickets to your game. They mentally want a seat. They are pulling for you. They're rejoicing in your success. Why? It is because you have connected them to your game, your vision. Think of all of the fans that could support your home team, your vision. In much the same way, you can attract people. Your vision, in a way, is their team. Your visionary result can make them ecstatic and exhilarated, because they are connected.

Vision is like a nucleus and the nucleus has the ability to capture nearby energy. The energy in this case is individuals. The nucleus itself may have limitations, but its surrounding energy is unlimited. What attracts that astonishing amount of energy is a shared vision. When the vision is clear, and it is chosen by the recipient to become a common denominator, someone that can create fulfillment, it's very gratifying for that member to be a part of that vision. Once that energy is created, it can overcome anything. It can overcome countries and cultures. Not only does it create the force of those people who are willing, but other people who are not part of the vision can still sense it and they are often amazed by the connection, the culture, the power, the movement, the flow and they are happy to be a part of it in whatever distant way.

What happens if you don't share your vision?

Think of it like a great idea. By not sharing it you immediately limit its potential. A great idea, like medicine, that you don't share is only going to help a confined area of people. However, by sharing it others can say "Hey I really need this. This is going to help." Or "We can add this chemical to eliminate this side effect." Or "We can use this system to distribute it". So you get endless input that is designed to the extension and development of a vision, simply by sharing it. Every time you advance your vision, you advance your energy, and the likelihood that your vision will occur. It will occur in a quicker period of time.

INPUT

The sharing part is very instrumental because of the openness, the transparency, and the willingness to ask for input. If you go about sharing your vision with an attitude of *this is our goal no matter what, and we can't tolerate any differentials,* energy does not have the freedom to grow. You might end up with the exact vision you started with, but to ask an opinion; *how do you feel about this? This is where we are headed, would you edit any part of this?* That takes the guardedness away, and invites the creative energy of others. The more times that it is tested, the more minds you get involved. People feel better connected when they know they have helped. Sharing will generate ideas to enhance your vision as time goes by.

Input is a form of glue. When you share your vision and ask for input and they say, "I want to be part of this" or "I have an idea". They are putting their glue toward your vision and that glue really sticks! The way they become part of it is through input. The more definable your vision, the more they will understand, connect, and commit to the end result.

CONNECTION

Connection is a big area where companies fail, and you can take it to any level. Let's say you give an assignment or understand what your job is; it's clear, it's definable etc. There is no connection, which is created partially by the input. If the connection does not exist, you have weakened the whole philosophy. In a case where you are trying to engage others in the visionary ending, we want to simply believe that everything is great, but we have to confirm that connection. They have to understand the vision. They have to contribute. Do you understand the vision? Yes. That is not a strong connection. We just want to get on to the next thing. We want to delegate it so bad, or we want to transfer the result performance elsewhere without making sure that it works. Just giving people work to do is an inefficient process. When you are talking about vision you have to create connection. The stronger the connection is, the more powerful the result.

All that energy is wasted if they don't know what the vision is or they don't feel they have a specific relationship to the vision. They are just doing a job or making a quota. Even though it may seem like a goal, it is not a common shared vision. That is why the magnetic force is so important to understand. When companies create an agenda with an intention and allow participants to design an intention that is completely harmonious with the company's intention it intensifies the connection and magnifies the result. My vision becomes our vision, our idea; our objective. When you share your vision with others, you also connect them with the power of vision. Not everyone is aware that they too have visionary powers and talents.

BELIEVERS

Believers are the people that have officially connected. They come into play and they want to take part. They are saying, *I want to be part of it. How can I be part of it?* Those are believers. If they don't know how to be part of it, they are just being honest. Believers are advanced connectors, like DNA strands that want to be connected to make the vision improve and come to pass. Often times they are just waiting for a connection to attach themselves. When your vision is clear you will attract more believers. The people you are going to attract are players and leaders. They are contributors. They are effective, credible people with a history of success that will be loyal during the creation process and beyond. That is a benefit of going through the visionary process. They are not all coming to the table the first time you say, *this is my vision come sign up.* They are always out there. They are kind of waiting for the bell to ring. That is when they will come. There are numerous people of this level just waiting for your visionary ring. It's time for you to tap the bell and attract these extraordinary contributors.

PROVISION

It's okay to begin sharing and making it public to your immediate network; which is not a big number for most people. It is usually a number fewer than 20. Even with a smaller number, how much more effective, powerful, and energetic is your vision when it is shared with that number versus being self-contained? Whatever your number is, if it goes beyond you then it has unlimited possibilities. When you don't initiate others into your vision, you will start to lose the energy. When you connect those people, they likely have either elements or energy. You are either building energy or losing energy. Which direction do you want to go? Sometimes it's a provisionary element; meaning a substance for your vision. Think about the word provision. You can break it down into pro and vision, meaning supporting the vision. You say, "I am looking to get my son a bike." Then someone says, "My father owns a bike store, and he would be happy to help." The substance, in this case, is not a creation; it is a substance that is always there. It is a combination of a person and the supply. Every supply needed for your vision either already exists or is ready to be created for your use. The interim step is to gather or create the element.

Most people think they have to go out and buy the substance, find the substance, or make the substance, but it's already there. There are exceptions, but many times it is readily available for you. If you said, "Gee, I need to get a book on astrophysics" and you hear, "Someone is moving and they are getting rid of a bunch of books." That may be the initial response. You have to share with more people, because then you hear, "My friend works at NASA and he has a bunch of books they aren't keeping anymore, he'd be glad to send you 10 or 12." Who knows, he might send you 10 every three months. That's provision. The provision can't expand until the vision is shared. Provisions are endless. Try it, it's free!

It is the concentric circle mentality. You can think of it like a radio beacon. It is not just a circle, but it is a living thing. It is a vibrating membrane. What does that mean? Well, I've expanded

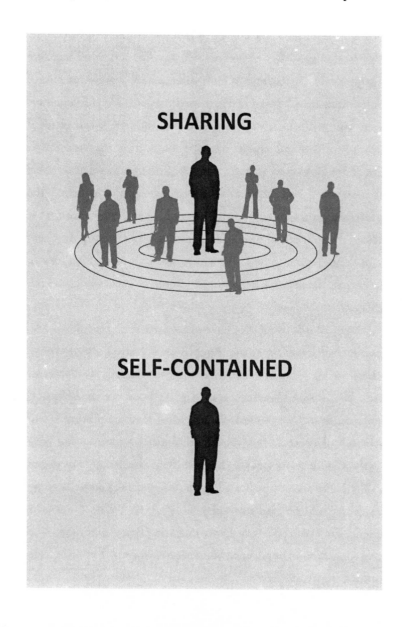

three, four, five rings outside my network to someone who I vaguely know through a connection. If something comes their way, they are vibrating and it will stick to them like glue, or orbit. They have no news, no provision, no elements, and no energy; they are just aware. If they are vibrating, those elements will stick to them. Suddenly something flies by them or they hear something. Then there is a new person, a new provision that entered in because of the vibration. It doesn't have to operate through you directly. It could be through anyone in the concentric circles. They become webs for any type of information or provision that happens to be flying in their space. They will catch it in their web and you will now have it. Your space to catch provisions is always expanding. Before, your space was only big enough to catch a finite amount but now your space has expanded so you can capture infinite amounts.

Whatever you want to bring into existence you can, if there is enough time. Chances are that anything you want to do; access to an element, a person, an executive, it already exists. So the question is, can you share your vision enough that it leads you into this desired position that you want? It is already there. Somebody you know, who knows somebody, who knows somebody else will eventually get you there. It is not a favor or begging. It comes through sharing. The unique part is the provision that you thought you needed comes to you better than you ever imagined. It should be expected, not hoped for. There is a big difference.

Sharing the vision needs to be watered and nurtured regularly. It's not like you can just share your vision once a year at a retreat or one time at a national conference. It is something that is repeated, nourished and discussed. You are constantly acting as a beacon for your vision. Its energy is passed around and the people are invited to add to the solution, the direction, the construction and the creation of how the vision will come to pass. That is what creates the dynamic forces of energy that can literally accomplish anything.

Chapter Five

PREPARATION

PREPARATION AND SUCCESS

I believe that preparation is 90% of success. Most extraordinary results were born from significant preparation. Take the highest paid athletes and entertainers and ask them how much time they give to preparation. You'll find it's a stunning amount, though it is done behind the scenes. Tremendous preparation is responsible for the creation of all multi-billion dollar industries. In fact **every successful person or company evolved from vision and preparation.**

PREPARING FOR THE OPPORTUNITY

Opportunities are going to occur. I heard a preacher once say that it is better to pray to be prepared for an opportunity than pray for an opportunity. If an opportunity comes along and you are not ready, then you are likely to underachieve. In life, you will get your share of big deals that pass your way; whether a marketing deal, manufacturing deal, or consumer deal. Those that are better prepared will have significantly stronger odds to win the deal. However, another key advantage is that **preparation breeds opportunity.** There is a magnetic pull here that leads to more opportunities that you will master.

Many of you have experienced the job interviewing process. Preparation here is very important and increases your chances of getting the job. Let's take a look.

Joe has an interview on Wednesday at the ABC Corporation. In preparation for the interview he defines his intention for the interview, reviews and improves his resume, picks out a nice suit, researches the ABC Corporation, researches and prepares to answer questions that may be asked in the interview, and asks for help and suggestions from people in his connection chain. Joe is prepared to exhibit confidence in his potential role at ABC Corporation.

Now Bob has an interview the same day for the same position at ABC Corporation, but he does not make the same preparations as Joe. Instead, Bob goes to the interview with an old copy of his resume. He knows nothing about the ABC Corporation, has not reached out to anyone in his connection chain, is unprepared for the questions, and thinks it is best if he just "wings it". Both Joe and Bob have the same opportunity, but which is best prepared? Who do you think will get the job?

You might be asking, what does this have to do with Strategic Visionary Planning? An opportunity's fruit is largely associated with your preparation. Preparation is defined as readying beforehand for a purpose, activity, or use. When you prepare for your definable intentions, your preparation will win.

Preparation is critical at the start, but it has continued importance and aspects for what is to follow. This is a continual process before every meeting, call, or project. Preparation wins! **Remember, vision is the definable intention from which preparation is formed.** This is what separates greatness from mediocrity.

THE MEETING PROCESS

Having a meeting is different than preparing for a meeting. Most meetings are completely inefficient and begin to evaporate moments after its conclusion. To create perpetual inspiration it is necessary to have a united vision of what the meeting results will yield. A preparation suggestion is to have you, or the entire team, write down what you want to result from the meeting in terms of measurability, tangibility, and timeline. Following the meeting you will know if you won or lost. You deal with the reality and not bureaucracy. Plus, there is accountability. Vision can be monitored and measured for its tangible points with related due dates. The more you practice vision and preparation, the stronger your results, and more obvious your superiority is witnessed. It also keeps you poised for fresh opportunities. It's all preparation.

Preparation is about winning the day. Remember, being busy does not equal success. You might feel like you're slammed, but in reality you're making tracks like a bear and not getting anywhere. Taking time to prepare gives you an advantage. Life seems to be inundated by meetings and various forms of communications. Many of these communications, in essence, are empty, vague, and inefficient unless someone takes the time to define the intention, prepare and have the courage to measure what they accomplished. Otherwise it is a cloud of inactivity, which is why most of the world fails. Results equal success and preparation is 90% of success.

BEFORE THE MEETING

Let's say you have a meeting with a prospective customer. What is your first step in preparing for the meeting? Normally people think about what they are going to present at the meeting. They will prepare all the items for what they want to cover. Doesn't everyone do this? Isn't this expected and ordinary? The more genius and productive approach is to determine the intention for the meeting. What are the exact results you want to see at the end of the meeting? Will there be a transfer of funds at the end of the meeting, a follow-up meeting scheduled, or will you solidify a business alliance at the end of the meeting? Whatever your intention may be, define it first. Once you know the intention then you will be more informed on what you need to prepare in order to achieve it by the end of the meeting. Without preparation, the meeting is wasting your time and others while the prepared person is extending their lead on the competition.

Let's say your intention is to get the prospect to commit to 1000 units by the end of the meeting, and give you one referral for 500 units in new business in the next 30 days.

This clear understanding directs your energy and preparation toward your definable result. If you have a team attending the meeting with you then it is important that everyone on your team understands and agrees to the purpose of the meeting. If your team does not have a common goal then you are not on the same team. It makes for a much better game when the team shares the intention. Let's win the game by accomplishing your predetermined intention. Then comes the preparation; make calls to people in your connection chain, and ask them what they have done in similar meetings. Study the topics, define the intention, note the points that you want to make, prepare to answer questions they may have, and determine your follow-up.

MEETING TIME

Start the meeting by asking questions. Find out what their needs are, what is important to them, and what they want to accomplish. Take good notes. Note what you think is important, but extra is better. This is your opportunity to win them over because they realize that they don't have all the answers to the questions. Winning a client or customer over for life is very important to the success of any business.

Your focus should still be on your predetermined vision. You may notice their answers align with your vision. The answers they don't have can be filled in with your vision, and you will connect them through their own admission as to what they want. It is a way for both of you to accomplish your visions. If their vision is not connected to yours in some way then it may not be a good fit. Look at the meeting as one of your initiatives. Can you improve the initiative or should it be discarded? This keeps it in the right container. The spirit of that is very positive, because you are connected to the energy. Almost always, it's a free source of energy effort toward your vision, and vice versa. Is anyone taking advantage of anyone? No. If it works, both parties will be happy.

Your focus should always be on directing the energy toward your vision; otherwise you are just a component. In life, we are all components of something, but we can be visionaries of anything. Maybe you just want to be a component or you want to be involved in visionary processes. It's like building a house. The architect already knows what the house is going to look like. Today he meets with the plumbers; tomorrow he meets with the electricians and the carpenters. He knows every dimension and function of the proposed house. Maybe the plumber, electrician and carpenter don't know what it's going to look like in the end, but they know their specific contribution. You might be surprised to find that by using this approach, the other party in the meeting will precisely replicate your predetermined result for the meeting. The best preoperational result is when others feel that they arrived at your result by their own admission, which is what you wanted.

AFTER THE MEETING

Stay bold after the meeting. It is important to take some time to go over what happened. Did you achieve your intention? If not, did it bring you any closer? Are the needs of the other party conducive to your vision? If a follow-up meeting was scheduled make notes about what preparations you need and what you want to accomplish in your next meeting. Because you were prepared and bold enough to measure your preparatory vision to the end result, you can now stay bold and make notes on what improvements are necessary for the next meeting. You should constantly be seeking this improvement. Pretty soon, as you continue meetings with this format, everyone will learn the importance of having an objective to meet during the meetings. **This separates winners from mediocrity, and entrepreneurs from worker bees.**

HOLLYWOOD MOVIE APPROACH AND YOUR STARDOM

There is a level of organization involved, especially when you are preparing for a meeting, event, or production that has a lot of moving parts. Your goal is to have everything fall into place perfectly so that you get the maximum results of your intention. To simplify this process, I use the Hollywood Movie Approach.

The average Hollywood movie lasts approximately one and a half hours. What you don't realize when watching the film is how much time and preparation goes into the final movie. The process of writing, casting, production, editing, and releasing a movie can take six months to two years. Why? It is because every part of the movie is rehearsed, and every part of the movie has an intention; even down to the inflection, emotion, and pacing of the dialogue. How much better would anything you did for an hour and a half be if you took two years to prepare? I am not saying that all 90-minute meetings, events, or productions need two years of preparation; but every minute of preparation can make the result significantly better.

Hollywood is a great example of a multi-billion dollar industry focused around an immense amount of preparation. They are not only prepared, but they continue to shoot the same scene until it's perfected. They are constantly improving. Preparation leads to perfection. Reading lines in a film is not a hard thing to understand. It does not seem complex, but they continue to reshoot takes to get it right. Many of the things that you do can also be improved through preparation. You think you understand them, but the repetitive practice, living it out on paper, and rehearsals only make you more effective when they call lights, camera, action!

Every part in the Hollywood Movie Approach is broken down into a segment or a section. The movie itself is usually broken down into three acts. You can apply the same logic to your event, meeting, call or production. A great example would be a seminar. Let's say you are a business person holding a seminar for prospective clients. Your intention is to get 10 new clients with specific criteria. Just like the movies, you can break it down into three acts

Once you break it down piece-by-piece, you see how all of the elements work together to create a successful event, and you become aware of improvements that need to be made. The more you do this process the easier it will be. Your events, meetings, calls, and productions should constantly be edited so that you can get to a higher and more efficient level. This keeps increasing the distance between your success and your competitors.

I believe in significant preparation, but even the smallest amount of preparation is an inspiration to the **power of time**. Give yourself a stronger advantage over those that do not take that time. Preparation not only saves the time of others, but also saves your time. Time is your biggest asset in life. As we learn how to extract energy, like nuclear energy from an atom, the power of time is even stronger. Preparation is an element to get that power and produce results.

ACT One- Prepare for Seminar

Scene 1- Find and book a venue.

Scene 2- Work with direct mailing company to send invitations to qualified prospective clients.

Scene 3- Confirm a professional to speak at your event about topics that concern your prospective clients.

Scene 4- Create an agenda for the event.

Scene 5- Work with a sponsor to help fund the event.

Scene 6- Confirm venue, attendees, professional speaker, and sponsor funds.

Scene 7- Rehearse the presentation.

ACT Two- Hold Seminar

Scene 1- The prospective clients arrive and are greeted by staff.

Scene 2- The speaker is introduced.

Scene 3- The speaker presents topic to prospective clients.

Scene 4- You are introduced.

Scene 5- You present to the prospective clients.

Scene 6- Information sheets are passed to the prospective clients and collected.

ACT Three- Seminar Follow-up

Scene 1- Gather notes about the event and any specific details you learned about prospective clients.

Scene 2- Thank the venue, speaker and sponsor for helping with a successful event.

Scene 3- Take appointments with the new prospective clients from the seminar.

Scene 4- Prepare for client meetings.

Scene 5- Close the new clients and seek referrals.

Scene 6- Review results from the seminar, and apply the information to your next event with new improvements.

Chapter Six

ANTI-VISIONARY PROCESSES

ANTI-VISIONARY PROCESSES

Anti-visionary processes are the things we do with our time that are counteractive to realizing our visions. There are many anti-visionary processes, but the two biggest ones are self-reliance and rabbit trails. There is an old saying, carpe diem, which is Latin for seize the day. What happens to people now is the opposite; diem carpe- the day seizes you. Many times the day just kicks your butt and steals your time. Your day can get so busy with emails, phone calls, notes, work and appointments. If you're so busy that you can't take 10 minutes before a meeting or a phone call to establish your definable intention or create power, and a few minutes afterwards to reflect your respective accomplishments, then plain and simple, the day seized you. Though you are being productive and being busy feels good, you won't come close to the highest level unless you direct the day's energy. We've all given away too many days. It's time to recapture what is yours.

RABBIT TRAILS

The more you understand about Anti-visionary processes the better you will be able to recognize and avoid them. Most of these come as friends or invitations, and appear to be harmless, yet they can yield destruction. Rabbit trails are the most common of anti-visionary processes. It is a proverbial term used to describe the act of going off the set path. When you author your vision, you create a pathway to victory. Pathways not directly aimed toward your vision are rabbit trails.

When I was growing up, I never heard the term A.D.D. which is commonly used to describe Attention Deficit Disorder. I think we all have that in some form. Advanced marketing, whether in television or in the stores, is designed to have you do impulse buying. It flashes alerts to attract your attention, which creates deviation to your pathway. Some of the products like coffee, soda, and cigarettes are intentionally designed for your addiction. They are capturing energy that implies you are going to support those products forever. The weird thing is when you get captured, and someone is watching you smoke or drink coffee, guess what? The watchers can become addicted or at least interested. That is the promoter's intention, and the inversed activity of your vision. Not only are you supporting those products with your own money, but you also are advertising for their imposed impulse. Is that the course you really wanted to go on? The answer is clearly no. These products are real, but symbolic of life's other temptations and traps.

For the first time in humanity, we are able to be in constant contact and have a world of information at our fingertips. The power of access to endless information and communication at the touch of a button can promote A.D.D. Should we have more communication? Sure. Should we have more constant information available? Yes. Should it distract you from your vision? No. Have you ever spent unnecessary hours playing a video game or surfing the web? These are good at times, but if over done will burn your productivity stockpile. Yes, more access can mean more rabbit trails. You can easily overcome A.D.D. by using the D.A.D. principle- Definable Intention, Accountability and Due Dates. See page 46.

Then there is the naked rabbit trail when there is no seeming distraction. You can't seem to get productive and simply not sure what to do. This is when you should start thinking about your vision more seriously; writing it, sharing it, and then experimenting. Some experiments don't work, but if you spend your whole life just experimenting then you end up being a rabbit trail tester. Some things that you think are good and aligned with your vision are not. Even things that are perfect, good, and aligned with your vision need to mature. Otherwise, every associated idea would be a success. Initiatives need to become more efficient and evolve in a higher mental form. This occurs by using people's alternative sources of energy that bring in new ideas, which you have to sort through and advance. Stay focused!

Rabbit trails can be subtle like the naked rabbit trail where nothing is going on or when you get into a routine. The routine is great if you are yielding visionary results, but people get married to their deficiently declining routines and say, *"My routine is good. I'm going to work every day, 10 hours a day. I'm on the phone. I'm responding to emails."* But at the end of that day you look and say, *"Hmm, there are no results here"* or *"I didn't plant any new seeds that will generate a great harvest in one week, one month, or one year."* If you make those statements, then your routine is wrong. Being busy does not win the day. There is no nice way to say it. You need to change. If you don't have a vision, and you're not willing to checklist your time, which is God's gift of your life, then you are not bold enough to examine your existence.

If you think about it, we are already visionary in many of life's activities. If we are going to the mall or the grocery store, we are thinking, *I'm going to the mall. I'm going to the grocery store.* On the way to the grocery store it is unusual you would go to the paint store, or go to a friend's house and never get to the grocery store. It could happen, but it is very unusual because you are set out to do something and you're going to do it. However, in vision, the "grocery store" is a little farther away and the distractions along that pathway are more tempting. There are promotions ringing out to you in the form of people, information, and entertainment which can be distracting. By the way, did you ever notice those who bring a list to the store have something to measure when they accomplish their shopping trip? While those that don't bring lists often forget all they want to accomplish during the shopping trip. The same principle applies in your visionary life. Without your written vision, you could forget numerous points that are integral and time saving.

How do I know it's a rabbit trail?

One way to know if it is a rabbit trail is to ask yourself, what am I going to yield from this activity? What is the harvest? If the answer is, I want to see what happens or this is just fun or everyone else is doing it then you know that it is probably a rabbit trail.

The problem with life today is rabbit trails are more prevalent than ever because of technology. With e-mail, internet, texting, and cell phones, we have the ability to skip around, sorting that information, and marry personal fun with business. Everybody wants to be in the loop, but sometimes being in the loop puts you in the seemingly inescapable orbit of rabbit trails. It becomes a little threatening. One way to deal with more choices is to allocate a section of time for those activities. Be strict and limit your involvement. Being in the communication loop all day is not only a symptom, but also confirmation that you are captured in the wrong orbit.

ENERGY ALWAYS SEEKS TO FIND A HOME

Energy always seeks to find a home. There are numerous types of energy which is always circling you and your pathway. The key is to attract the type you want and avoid all others. The more accomplished and versatile you are the more likely you are going to be bombarded with various forms of energy sources which can inefficiently consume your energy. Becoming more focused through a visionary process, your energy can be directed to sort that which is related to your vision and let you operate in a more perfect environment.

Imagine living in a house that has no windows on the window openings. All of a sudden you put a screen in the window openings. Window screens only keep animals and bugs out while the cold or the heat still gets in. So then you install a window and seal it. Pretty soon the only type of energy in the house, though it's all around outside of the house, is the energy you want, cool or warm and bug free. That is how we live our visionary lives; by screening invading rabbit trails. However many of us let our lives open to up to distractions where your own creative vision could be lost. Once again, it is confirmation that "Without vision the people shall perish", (Proverbs 29:18). The biggest reason why people don't reach tremendous heights is because they have been rabbit trailed to death. We get used to operating amidst the infection when clearly a more sterile atmosphere will produce higher results and longevity of success.

Think about how simple it is to author your own vision. Just like a child asking for a red toy truck for his birthday, it is very distinct and with a timeline. That is a simple thing, but most people haven't even done that. It's only symbolic to me that they have been consumed or are being consumed by outside energy forces on a daily basis to the point that their life doesn't have the preferred directions it was meant to enjoy.

TIME IS A GIFT

Rabbit trails can be overcome by first determining who is controlling the energy and if it is in tune with your vision. Winning each day, or as many as you can, has to have a measure.

You are accountable for the day. Did the day bring you closer to your vision or did you just simply work hard all day? Most people are involved in that type of living. The key is to hold yourself accountable by measuring the day. The days will vary and there can be volatility, but when you get in the habit of measuring your day it will bring you closer to your vision, and you will sense a greater satisfaction of your presence in life.

Time is the plasma when it comes to vision. Time and vision are gifts. If we spend our money on something that is non-functional, doesn't work, and not what we expected then we are quick to complain. We should treat time the same way, because time is more important than money. If in a period of time we don't receive the value for our time we should be complaining. The person to complain to, in this case, is yourself. We should hold ourselves accountable for this blessed gift; the **valuable asset of time**. We have all misused our time whether going along a wrong path, being inefficient, or curious. The process of Strategic Visionary Planning decreases those wastes, while increases the value and energy of time, making more of life's moments effective with long-term meaning.

Is it difficult to tell what a rabbit trail is, if you don't have your initiatives defined?

Rabbit trails will find you every day. They are random ideas, thoughts, other people's issues, energy that is directed somewhere else. At first, when you touch it, it seems like; Wow I can employ this energy to get to my vision. If it doesn't match up harmoniously, it's a rabbit trail. The fact is 90-99% of all the energy that approaches you every day is a rabbit trail until you become visionary. The percentages start to shift in your favor where that amount of energy is there to serve you. The outside negative energy realizes it's not getting anywhere, and your energy is growing and overcoming with definitive types of initiatives and passion that wants to be specifically directed toward the accomplishment of your vision.

SELF RELIANCE

The second most common anti-visionary process is self reliance. Many people rely too heavily on themselves. In other words, they think they are the only ones who can get the job done. You are the visionary and therefore the most integral part of your vision, but you cannot achieve the vision in a reasonable timeframe alone. In the rare cases that you can, you will lessen the future of expansion and acceleration. It is much easier to realize and incorporate the multifaceted masses of energy all around to help you achieve your vision more efficiently and eternally. Turn your self-reliance into perfecting and utilizing the strength of others, while you advance to the next phase.

The next time you have a big meeting, project or production, reach out to the people in your connection chain. They may not be in the same industry, but the logic can help. That is what I call expansion of the mind; **increasing the potential of your definable intention** and an example of you seizing the day all at the same time. Our intuitive mind would tell us to react to the situation and deal with the meeting, project, or production 100% personally. When you seek other people and go through that example of preparation you get a wide perspective, but you don't lose your intuitive talents. You still have your contributions, except they have now been widened to give you different dimensional perceptions, which make your original idea more effective. Still you, just better! This act of preparation allows you to deliver the result you sought.

Speaking arrogantly about your accomplishments or progress is also an example of self-reliant behavior. It seems easy to recognize your own accomplishments for what you inspired, but sometimes it's anti-visionary. What is visionary is to acknowledge anybody and any source that helped, because that gives you a key to access the energy of that person(s) and increases it. Whatever energy we have and whatever credit or recognition we deserve, it is far less than the expansions of the unlimited number of contributors who want to be part of a great vision. When you spend a lot of time saying *I built this house or I grew this business* you would be better off saying *how can I inspire other people and recognize them for what they have done to help my vision? What other energies can I capture?* Develop questions from this perspective instead of talking only about yourself. The greatest visionaries are not the foreman type that micromanage everything, instead they are delegating, educating, expanding, and utilizing all resources. This frees them to think at a higher level while inviting the participation of others.

We get caught up in all of our capabilities and the singleness of what we are, which can be anti-visionary. We have that whether or not we broadcast daily. You can be the captain of the ship to accomplish the definable result, but vision is the compilation of using other energy sources.

PERCEPTION OF IMPROVEMENT

Sometimes we get caught in the trap of thinking the process is good enough. It's big enough, completely developed, and it works fine. This is complacency, which is another anti-visionary process. Even if it is good in your assessment, it can always be improved. There are no exceptions. Anything that is could be better and most things are better because of continued improvements. Even the source of nourishment can be better, which is to say that even what makes it better can also be improved. Think about the evolutions in technology. What if we stopped improving cell phones in 1995? We would not have all the amazing features and efficiencies that we do today. Even now, should we stop improving cell phones? They occurred because there was a perception of improvement. Vision wants to be better. It needs to be better. In this sense, everything wants to evolve in the dynamics of vision to be bigger and stronger. That is the inherent purpose of that energy source, and it needs and wants the chance to flourish. This theory applies to everything you can imagine.

It's like opening up a restaurant because everyday 16 buses stop at this particular corner. So you build the restaurant there and say, "Wow, this is unbelievable! The buses are going to stop here. I'm going to put a sign on the corner. They are going to love me. I'm going to have a constant source of customers." Then suddenly, the buses stop coming because the route was changed. Now what? In visionary planning, it is you who make the buses come. You were reacting to a situation versus creating the specific one you wanted. Creating results you want is visionary. Vision is not only creative, but also attractive. You attract the buses. You have a fuel stand, a bus cleaning service, a restaurant. You have an attraction for the buses. It doesn't matter what you are trying to attract whether it is buyers, buses, or businesses you can create the situation and they will come.

KEEP YOURSELF MOTIVATED

Individuals will find a way to excite themselves, get motivated, and then sometimes the passion drifts away. It is like a fleeting moment of gratification. Keeping yourself motivated is the best anti-rabbit trail device. Now sometimes it is difficult to keep yourself motivated. For example, when you are trying to lose weight you think, *I'm going for a walk today and I won't eat anything bad.* It's hard to bear that, but it is easier to bear it when you have help. People have trainers, sign up at the gym, or go with a friend. Having help and someone to walk with you is a big plus. That is true in business and life too. When you are trying to motivate yourself in business or in general, you have to make a list of motivating people, motivating books, motivating phrases and other people who want to be motivated with you, people who will encourage you, so you bring more of the desired result. Like vision, bring more of that energy near you to create endurance.

We have listed some of the anti-visionary processes. Most of these perishable processes come to a sad ending. In this world, you are either employing energy or wasting its availability. There isn't really a middle area. There are cases that maybe you can slow down the deterioration process, but in general you are either increasing your creative concentric circles or you're decreasing them. You can decrease them at a slower rate so you don't think they are perishing, but it is just a mediocre way to an eventual end.

AVOID ANTI-VISIONARY PROCESSES

You can avoid anti-visionary processes by dissecting your vision and asking,

Did I plant the seeds of my definable intention?

What did I generate?

Did I use the template and the D.A.D. principle as my guide?

How many others did I inspire to participate, and did they inspire anyone else?

Be aware and focus on theses protective mechanisms. Have your team do the same. If you can't answer these questions, then maybe you have wasted your time. So even if you had a lousy day, week, or month you can still have one that is 10 times better. Your focus should be to make it multiply; where the identifiable results equal the definable intentions. If the identifiable results don't equal the definable intentions, you're on a rabbit trail. You have to ask yourself, *do I want to be a part of my dreams and vision, or do I just want to be in a pool of misplaced, random energy that has no destination?* **Your vision is your pathway to victory.**

Chapter Seven

CONNECTION CHAIN

ENERGY HAS A NAME

Everyone is gifted. In the field of vision, we are all amazing, only in different ways. Each one of us has a type of energy. Some inspirational, some as a key link, some as the inspiration to improvements, and hundreds of other wondrous parts. There is also genius. There are people that have pure genius, and there are people who have genius in a categorical sense. Some have organizational genius, some have entrepreneurial genius, some have accounting genius, some have communicative genius, and so on. The point is that the power of all of this genius energy has a name. It's the name of someone you know. It's the name of someone you're going to know. It's the name of someone who you know, knows. You will have access to not only your talent, but the genius of others. Much of this genius will contribute to your team and achievement of your vision.

CONNECTION CHAIN

Vision has a strong gravitational pull that is not so different from that of the sun, the moon and the earth. You can create that gravitational pull. Incidentally, people can be pulled into a gravitational force against their knowledge or will, while others desire to be pulled. People need direction, a home, a source. They want to be connected to something that is credible and solid; a place that they feel gratified. They want to be part of something. Self-actualization!

You now understand that sharing is one of the most important stages in Strategic Visionary Planning. The more you share, the more orbiting objects you create, the more powerful your universe. If you connect others to your vision, they will share your vision with the people they know and it will perpetuate itself. This creates your gravitational pull. We discussed perpetual energy earlier in the book. You have access to all the energy and resources that exist, it is just a matter of plugging into them. It does not happen overnight. What does happen overnight is a stirring, a creation, or birth. This quickly becomes visual proof of the power of your vision.

Think of the connection chain like a redwood tree. The redwood is a mighty tree. Its roots do not grow straight into the ground. They grow horizontally, and tie into other redwood roots. One tree becomes many with the strength of all of the redwoods. A tree has a base known as the trunk. Think of yourself as the tree trunk. Attached to the trunk are branches. Think of those branches as the people you know. Each branch has smaller subsequent branches attached to it, and smaller branches attached to even smaller branches until you get to the smallest branches and twigs. Those branches and twigs symbolize the people who you know, knows. The point is you are connected to all of it. Just because the twig is not directly attached to the trunk does not mean they are not connected. Together, all of those pieces make up a tree. Every tree needs air and water. It needs to be nurtured in order to grow tall and strong. So does your connection chain.

The connection chain is a process that I link to DNA. DNA are the building blocks of life. Visualize that each block or strand of DNA equals one element in your connection chain, and each of those elements makes up your vision. Not only are the strands of DNA capable of expanding, connecting and serving all, but as time progresses there is an improvement for each component and thus more powerful results evolve. Usually, you cannot build 20 elements in week one. It starts with one, two, three then grows to eight, twenty-two and it builds more and more. It is endless. You can cut it off at any place that you feel comfortable. You don't have to be the biggest operation in your community, but you can if that is your vision.

POWER IN NUMBERS

There is an old saying that two minds are better than one. Well, ten minds are better than two. It is not unreasonable to believe that we can have the power of two people or ten people. The potency of that is strengthened by the clarity of the vision. You can have 200 people. There is no limit. The key to aligning other people to your vision is the connection chain and sharing. People get excited about ideas, but they are just a puff of smoke. Then there are visionaries who are enthusiastic about their defined vision. The enthusiasm around the vision is catchy, and it is a constant gravitational pull for other energy. Sharing a clear vision attracts more people.

The American corporate world teaches people only to do their jobs and does not challenge or encourage them to be visionary. I would rather be the person with the revolutionary spirit than someone who just does what they are told. Even if you are undercapitalized, if you believe in your vision you have already won the biggest battle. When you hear someone say, "You have to listen to me because I have more than you", that represents one of the worst aspects in capitalism. Some business models take away the power of the people that appear less able to be superstars. In the visionary world, every player has the ability to increase their capacity. Thus, the definition of your vision opens the door to the accessibility of unlimited amounts of material supply. Your vision offers a refreshing opportunity to them. Yes, some may never have buildings with their name on them or make honors on the front page of the newspaper, but they can become exceedingly successful, because of your visionary inspiration. So why would you want to lose the energy of that exponential capacity and resource? This could mean without your vision, others may perish.

Atoms are a good example. Some atoms are very weak, but when you mix them with another weak chemical it becomes a bond or it becomes a very potent formula. That's how it is with people. You can take a person who doesn't seem to have the greatest abilities, or certainly make the statement that this person is not going to end up a superstar. However, that person could end up as a major relative force in getting others to do certain things that are unfathomable to believe from the beginning. I have seen it many times. People older in age suddenly hit the apex of their career, not because they got lucky or they went back to school, but because they got the opportunity to be part of something that is definable. Visionaries do this! It is such a powerful thing. Why wouldn't you want to give someone that chance? Your vision will not only be self-fulfilling, but it will reward others for being connected. You will be forever commemorated for expanding your vision to offer opportunities for others to excel!

START WITH THE DEFINABLE INTENTION

Building your connection chain is an enjoyable process. You can have tremendous fun, access a mass of benefits, and immerse yourself in a great assortment of talent, while obtaining your dreams. The great part is it is free!

The visionary template replicates itself like cells of life. Each cell or combination serves a purpose for the support of life. Similarly, it is important to understand your systemic chain. When vision takes its true form, and the connection chain is utilized, your vision will align itself to reach your definable intention.

HELPING PEOPLE

Your connection chain is made up of two sections of people; helping people and people helping. Though their names are similar they serve different functions. Helping people are the people that you want to help, and will benefit from your product or service. People helping are the people who help you help the people you want to help. That is a lot of helping!

Building your connection chain works by identifying and defining, as specifically as you can, the people that you are trying to help. For example, do you want to help the elderly, cancer

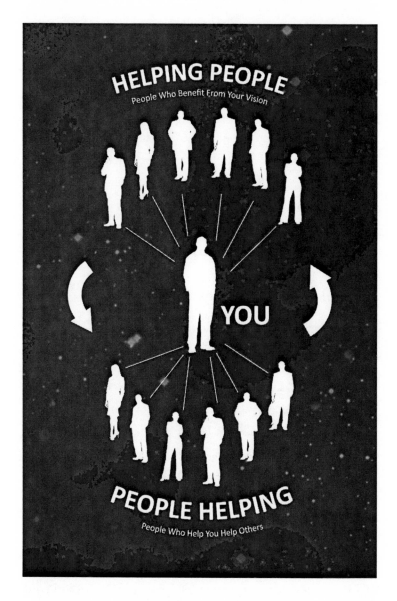

patients, business owners, or consumers? Who are you trying to help? These are the helping people. Secondly, who can help you help those people; organizations, friends, businesses, marketing companies? Those people can help you.

When we get older we operate on expectations, and historical structure. This is completely contrary to vision. Let's say you have a client and you tell your client that you want to help them, and you want to help them in this way. You want to provide them something. You want to be available. Whatever it is, you want to help. You have to define that, just as you define your vision. Do you want to provide a product or service? Do you want to be friends with them? What are the definable ways that you want to help them? Sometimes we don't know how we want to help and that is okay. This is where we exercise sharing and input. Ask them how you can help.

On the next page is an illustration of a "Helping People" list and you decide who goes on that list. You have to identify the people you want to help and how you want to help them.

Now think about your vision. Are you helping people? Identify the helping people relative to your vision.

From there you make a list of people who are related or have contact with those people. There are probably other people trying to help that same group, but in a different capacity. These are the people helping. Ask yourself, can you help people all alone? The answer is no. Maybe you can help them, but wouldn't you want to provide them and yourself the best and most efficient resources? Think about who can help you, help them. Do you have an assistant? Do you have a marketing department you could call? Do you have a wholesaler you can call? Pretty soon you will discover that you now have people. Eventually, you will be able to identify these people as winners and drivers.

Think about your list of helping people. Who can help you help them? Identify the people helping relative to your helping people.

Helping People

Who Can I Help?	How Can I Help?
1. Business Owners	Manage their business finances
2. Affluent Clients	Manage their money and exceed their return expectations
3. Bob, Products Advisor	Increase sales for his division
4. Two Finance Students	Provide a $5000 college scholarship

Your connection chain can get so big that you can't handle the outpouring of energy that you sought out from the beginning. When you seek to help people, you can't escape the

Helping People

Who Can I Help?	How Can I Help?
1.	
2.	
3.	
4.	
5.	
6.	
7.	
8.	
9.	
10.	

byproduct of the fact that others will become connected; if they sense that helping is your mission. When the essence of your connection is to help, it becomes evident to the people you

People Helping

Who Can Help Me?	How Can They Help Me?
1. Mary- Marketing Professional	Reach business owners in the community using an effective marketing campaign
2. James- Customer Service Specialist	Facilitate better business practices for maximum client retention
3. Bob- Products Advisor	Implement the best products on the market to help my clients
4. Jack- Banker	Finance business expansion plan
5. Anna- Support Staff	Manage current and new clients effectively with a 98% retention rate

are trying to help and the people helping you. Your intention becomes magnified. Therefore it makes you much more unique and genuine than someone who is simply trying to get business.

People Helping

Who Can Help Me?	How Can They Help Me?
1.	
2.	
3.	
4.	
5.	
6.	
7.	
8.	
9.	
10.	

Normally, the connection chain boils down to, or should boil down to, attracting and nourishing its members. It is not about the money, it's about the people! Whether a doctor, teacher, police officer, businessman, or a sales person, these people have talent and are willing to share. All visionaries help people either directly or indirectly. People trying to help others want to share ideas. These people have greatness that can be expanded.

Is vision only for the sake of helping people?

Yes, and you're the first person it helps. Your vision may seem materialistic with a financial goal or have some specific finite objective that seems personal. It has that right. You are authoring the future. However, along the journey helping people, particularly those that participate or maneuver in your energy field are obvious beneficiaries. Even if it was not your original intention, helping people in a variety of ways is what occurs. It may help them financially, get a job, or psychologically connect them to something they feel has meaning. Ultimately, they become a real part of the valuation or equity you establish. Bonus opportunities exist for all along the pathway. Surely and truthfully it gives people a fresh viewpoint and perception they didn't have before your visionary invitation. It's an additive to people's lives that starts with your vision.

WINNERS AND DRIVERS

Winners and drivers are twofold. The first group are those that are proven winners and drivers. You can identify that there are experts in and out of your field. You can find winners and drivers that are experts in marketing, communication, closing a sale etc. It is very important to identify those that already exist and gather information from their experiences. This asset and tool is a blessing to you in realizing your vision.

Your vision's clarity will also attract a percentage of talent with a great capacity to learn. These individuals can develop into winners and drivers necessary for success. Your vision waters them. Identification is a starting point for connection and measurement of the future. Finding the right person at the right place is not always obvious. Your job is to connect them to a result that is definable, for which they are accountable with a due date. Remember the D.A.D. principle, which stands for Definable intention, Accountability, and Due date in written format.

How do I Improve My Connection Chain?

Every time you increase your shared specifics, the end result becomes a lot more possible, more powerful, and long lasting. It is very similar to why we have wiring in a house and not just one wire. It's specific; this wire goes to living room; that wire goes to kitchen; and another wire goes to the garage. Numbers make it simple and can be sectioned off as you determine who can plug into each part and its relative function.

Connection chains, like winners and drivers, are made *like a cake, a house or a magnificent enterprise. The cool part is it doesn't matter where you are now, but in a very short period of time you can start* *the linkage, which can expand and accelerate. Once started, the links of your connection chain can be endless. Eventually, everyone in your connection chain can know everyone necessary to access the abundant power to deliver more than you require. It's a spiritually-based power, and the spirit is to help people! Subsequently, you have access to the best energy. You become a resource, and more result-oriented people are coming by your desk for enlightenment. You can build that from a dead stop to being the number one in your city, state or world. Most people not using this format are led by short-term urges, greed or by forfeiting the helping of others. That may seem like a logical point of view, but it doesn't differentiate you from the thousand competitors you have within a 30-mile radius. What differentiates you is the spirit of the connection chain that you are driving. Once again you are surpassing the norm.*

THE MATH MAKES SENSE

Sue, who works at ABC Financial Resources, has identified that she wants to help small businesses. It is her niche. So of course she wants to get in front of small business owners. She connects with the marketing department and says she wants to get in front of business owners. The marketing department gives her a list of 10 advisors who deal with business owners. Now she has names and phone numbers of 10 advisors who already do what she wants to accomplish. How simple is that? Sue takes 10 minutes to call each advisor, less than two hours of her time. Well worth it. How much experience and vital points is Sue going to learn in that time? I'll estimate 100 years. She calls the other advisors and says, "I hear you deal with small business owners. Tell me your experience. How do you market? What are the pros and cons? You're a business owner, how do you feel?"

Sue isn't selling anything, nor trying to get them to move. She is just requesting their professional and helpful comments. The more input they give, the more their connection. After she's talked to several of the other advisors and taken notes, she decides to call a wholesaler. In the financial industry, wholesalers are always trying to meet with advisors just like pharmaceutical reps want to meet with doctors and so on. Sue calls a wholesaler and asks, "What products do you have that serve the small business owner?" They give her the name of a company. Now Sue can call that company to get all of the information. By now, Sue has connected with 10 advisors, a wholesaler, and a company that can help her provide services to her clients; the small business owners. Within these short mentoring calls, Sue has been energized with new intellectual resources.

Now how long do you think it took for Sue to make those calls; a couple of hours maybe? How much money did she spend? Zero. How much do you think those intellectual resource will help her vision and help others? The answer is massively. Do the math. Zero cost equals massive results.

It does not matter what industry you are in or what you are trying to accomplish, you can apply this technique to anything. An important point to remember is to take notes, and thank them for their input. You may like an idea or hate it. You may modify it to your style. Their information is now in your library. They're helping you and subsequently helping others. Your connection chain is being watered and you will see it begin to grow.

How can I expand my connection chain if I'm an introvert?

The visionary process is a lesson and education for Strategic Visionary Planning throughout your life. So if you're shy, timid and you don't want to aim for the highest possible end result, it's okay. Start the process anyway and you will still see amazing achievements. You will learn how to utilize this process, and gain a little bit of confidence. You will feel the energy. If you are sensitive to what you are creating, and sensitive to the energy that is around it, you will be more in tune with the power that you have, and it will create more confidence. You will think, wait a minute I can almost get an energy meter and measure that the energy has increased since I began. Each time you are in a visionary process, your personality might not change, but your confidence and results of what you are accomplishing will noticeably increase.

Energy has a name and vision is the beginning of a destination that has a roster of people who are going to participate. Vision will bring it together. It is just waiting for your inspiration. That start button is you. When you are seeking a specific name of energy or type of energy, just ask. For example; who is a great sales person? Who is a great closer? Who is a great marketer? How can we create more inspiration? How can we create more connection?

How can we create more names to speak with? Asking these kinds of questions is a great start. You don't know all the names yet, but by passing that out into your field, the names will start suddenly appearing, because someone somewhere has that talent. Even if no one person has the greatest talent to solve it completely, the sum of the voltage of the energy of each person will equal more than the total needed for that particular question. The burden of the completed project is not just on you. What is on you is the beginning and so you have to press the start button. The accessible energy comes from the connection chain. Just by asking them you have gathered more mental giants to help you. The questions themselves inspire the connection. The real secret behind that is sharing the definable intention with energy sources in the form of questions, thoughts, and opinions from them. Soon you will see that energy has a name. There are many people with your desired talent or resource. Perhaps no one has the full talent to serve your vision completely, but the sum of the energy in your connection chain will equal more than what is needed. Remember this: Energy has a purpose and energy follows the intention of the result.

Chapter Eight

PERPETUAL ENERGY

PERPETUAL ENERGY

Perpetual energy is the fuel that your strategic visionary plan utilizes. It is just like the power outlets in your home. You can plug any piece of equipment into the outlet, and it will function. This outlet is capable of handling any size power, need or vision. The power is already there. Just like vision, the power is available to everyone. The power is indiscriminate. The outlet doesn't know if Catherine, or Amanda, or Gordon is putting in the plug. It only knows that someone is requiring this energy, and the outlet connects you to the source. Though similar, our sources are not the outlets in the wall. Our source is every type of energy that human intelligence can access.

To know that the energy exists is one thing, but tapping into it is another. Be confident that there is more energy available than you could ever use. With so much power available, you must be wondering where to start? It's simple, start with one person or group at a time. Every time you share your vision you are encouraging ideas, positive communication, and defining goals. Creating perpetual energy is about being consistent and allowing energy to flow to your vision. The vision is the plug. You cannot just roll up the electrical cord when you think you are finished. You have to be ready to plug in your vision at any time.

START THE STARTERS

Start the starters means taking active energy that has been dormant to your cause and igniting it towards your vision. The problem is most people underestimate what their resources are. The fact of the matter is that you have access to almost every resource available. It's hard to say that because then people say, "Well, send me a million dollars." It is not instantaneous, but you do have that access. You have to identify who are your resources, connections, friends, and continue sharing your vision. Pretty soon you will see the expansion of resources available for your cause.

The first step is to make a list of individuals, companies, organizations, and any form of connection that you know. The second step is to make brief commentary on each connection's specialties. You will begin to see a lot of talent. How do you start the starters? The best way to approach a starter is by asking them questions about how they handle their niche. How many power sources does your connection chain know? Eventually it develops more starters, and this list becomes an endless energy force. How powerful the source varies by how much attention you give. You can start with, "I don't know anyone. I don't know a congressman. I don't know a business man." That's okay, because eventually all your resources lead to the specific power you need. Know that once you're in, you're in for bigger measure. Vision does not expand and accelerate when you leave it in a box. So why not press the start button?

Think about your vision and list the individuals, companies, organizations, and any other connection whose energy is waiting to be ignited towards your vision.

Start the Starters List

Name	Functions and Success
1. Jane G.	Top marketing executive
2. Stephen A.	Expansion Expert
3. Dennis R. Imagine Products	Mergers
4. Diane S.	Single Product
5. Allen W.	Franchising
6. Charles D. JC Plus 1, Inc.	Multiple Service
7. Kevin S.	Outside Distribution
8. Michael S. Jack's Solutions	Product Manufacturer

When you author your vision you become this center point of energy. It's transferable, because it is simple to understand. I want to help 1000 senior citizens have a stable financial future by the

Start the Starters List

Name	Functions and Success
1.	
2.	
3.	
4.	
5.	
6.	
7.	
8.	
9.	
10.	

end of three years. When you plug in and share then you can ask, "What are your thoughts? Who do you know who has done this? How would you improve this?" Then the people who you plug into will perpetuate that energy. They may say, "I have a friend who helps senior citizens," to someone they meet and speak with. It starts to perpetuate itself.

If you need access to all CEOs of all Fortune 500 companies, you can have access. Even if you were the most powerful CEO of that group, and you wanted to have access to all the other 499, you will be limited in doing so unless you use perpetual energy. It may be easier for certain people of certain power and certain status to get there faster and more efficiently. However, it is not restricted to them alone. You can perpetuate yourself into a position of higher resources, status power and quicker access to energy. Once you start perpetual energy that accessibility is available to anybody. That applies not only to Fortune 500 companies and business power, but any group with power. You want to perpetuate your energy into different groups and different sources. Start at the lowest level. The people perpetuating the energy in that particular source are married to the source. Those people also become married to your vision and they express it amongst the source. It's free advertising, free electricity in multiples. It is an unlimited amount of power. I have yet to see a person who, once they start to connect to that power, has the ability to even keep up with the supply. No one person's vision, in my experience, is beyond obtainable.

Every communication is a way to perpetuate energy, so you have to prepare. Keep your connection chain in front of the the numbers. Let them see status reports. It is key that your energy isn't me, me, me. The purity and simplicity is the most important part in sharing. Give them the opportunity to contribute input to your vision. You can check in with them a month later and say, "My vision is to help 1000 senior citizens have a stable financial future by the end of three years. We have been able to help 100 so far. I just want to let you know, because you took the time to listen to me before. I appreciate your time and input."

A bonding occurs and you create a connection and stay in their minds. It continues to perpetuate itself, because you have prepared yourself by having the vision and sharing. You don't know who they know, and the millions of people they are connected to. That is why you share with everyone, and perpetuate every source. Maybe that is why there are sports standings in the newspaper? So everyone can keep score.

You ignite the energy of others, which is constantly working and expanding even if you are not physically present. You were the big bang of this energy so to speak. Perpetual energy is a gift and gives you access to the energy and resources of others. Use your visionary template to transfer what results you are seeking to the energy sources of people. To transfer it is the key. You can pray about it quietly, talk about it, or write it down. Visuals are always the best to transfer. Writing and showing can occur in many different fashions. You can write them a note or just keep showing your visionary plan. All of those create energy.

In the beginning, you may only use part of the energy. Over time, you will use two, three, and five times as much. The people who understand perpetual energy end up having 100 times or 1,000 times more from where they started. It is easy to perpetuate, because of the simplicity of having a written vision. It is a sum of the pieces. Through careful preparation, perpetuating energy and illuminating others can give you access to more resources and inspire more outside energy to start working on your behalf. Sounds super powerful!

Having access to all of that energy can also create some issues. Since the energy is so powerful, you get numerous opportunities. Some are positive and some are not. It puts you in a diversification situation, and you have to be careful not to drift off onto a rabbit trail. The ability to stay focused and be close to your core vision is key in the expedience and the prominence of which your vision is fulfilled.

Remember that you have to approach it with confidence. **You can access this energy**. The visionary person who has the written, transferable, energy-gathering plug is also much more respected. It is unique. Most people will not hand out a written vision. When is the last time you handed someone your written thoughts? You have to believe in what you have written. Be proud of your vision and share it! Whether they help you or not doesn't matter. You are still going ahead regardless! You have to decide whether you believe in the power of this universe. There is talent and resources or there isn't. Once you decide there is, the rest is just plugging in. The plugging in is a constant process that you prepare for on a daily basis. Perpetual energy is a great way to win the day. During the day did you work your tail off? I know a lot of people who work their tail off and don't get the results they want. You can answer 200 emails a day, but if you are not perpetuating energy you are running on a treadmill. You are moving and getting nowhere. Perpetuate energy in whatever you do. Whether it's answering an email, requesting an energy return, or making a call to action, you will see the result. Every day can be won, and every day you win your vision multiplies and grows stronger in size and effectiveness.

If you want access to all the power, all the intelligence, and all the growing resources that exist then now is the time to get all the ingredients to reach your vision. **So start perpetuating.**

Chapter Nine

REPLACE YOURSELF

Replacing yourself is the final stage in Strategic Visionary Planning. It is like getting your diploma. This final stage brings you to the top. It is like taking all the courses, all the labs, doing all homework, partaking in all the activities, and not getting a diploma. Replacing yourself is like education; you can continue to get to higher levels and stature with Strategic Visionary Planning. I say it is the final stage because it is the level that creates the stabilization of your vision while offering leaders unlimited opportunity for expansion.

Many people have a difficult time understanding this stage. I get mixed reactions when I speak to people about replacing themselves. First, there is a group of people who feel that they are irreplaceable and if they replace themselves, they would have nothing left to do. They tend to have the mindset to keep things confidential and secretive so they protect themselves and their ideas. This falls into the anti-visionary process of self-reliance. This is where most everyone is now. You should have seen many along your journey. They are essentially saying they have no desire to improve and learn because they hold captive all the keys of development. Yet, they don't.

The other group of people is learning, spirited, passionate and aggressive, but they don't know that they can replace themselves or they just have no clue what they would do if they did replace themselves. This type is more willing to replace themselves they just don't know where to start. The fact is you don't always have to have that clue. Replacing yourself helps everything work better. It does not mean that you trust everyone and leave the venture. Replacing yourself still requires leadership, but a more fun and higher level of leadership. Isn't that what you really want? It's kind of like taking the roof off of the operation and seeing the bigger picture. It becomes clearer how things can work more efficiently by having someone else who is passionate and highly-spirited in charge of a certain area. You may not replace yourself as a whole at first, but you may have replacements in the categorical sense. Earlier in the book, we talked about other people having categorical genius, and developing them into leaders. Replacements come in with a new passion to learn, improve, mentor, and be mentored. While they are taking over with that kind of intensity, you are free to think of something else at a higher level. Yes, you guide them, but you have now created more time for yourself and time is your greatest asset. You usually end up going into some kind of leadership observational role. New challenges will arise as you lead your replacements. You will become more effective leading than doing. You don't always have to see yourself in that next stage first unless it was initially a visionary focus. It is simplest to pick a category or area where you want to replace yourself. Maybe it's making calls, processing paper work, or regular negotiations.

Replacing yourself may be the final stage in Strategic Visionary Planning, but it does not mean that you leave it for the end. You should start immediately. Remember, it does not have to be a full-scale replacement. Someone has to make the initial contacts, do the first stage of negotiations, and follow-ups. So starting to replace yourself immediately is the impetus that lifts you to the next highest level. Why wouldn't you want that to start in the beginning?

A great thing about replacing yourself is it creates a kind of insurance if something were to happen to you. The whole operation would not fall apart, especially if you have replaced yourself categorically with multiple people or departments. You are stronger immediately.

WHO SHOULD REPLACE ME?

You are never going to know 100% or even 70% if you have found the right person to replace you, but the question is, is it the right time? I am a believer that leaders are made, not born. If you have good leadership abilities and your candidate is able, passionate and spirited, you should be able to get something out of that replacement. Unless you are in a specific field like law or accounting that requires certain skills and education, you are better off finding someone that you can mentor. Even in those cases, chances are you can still find a candidate to mentor. If it isn't the right person then that is okay. You can move on to the next candidate.

When you look for someone to replace yourself you do not need a carbon copy of yourself. Yes, it is good to have someone who has your intellectual capabilities, but most likely their style will be different. That can be a great thing, because it brings a different perspective. You already have your perspective. Why not get another? The most important thing is that they are passionate, results-oriented, and have a good work ethic.

How do I give up control?

When you have the desire to overly control you have to ask; is that impulse controlling you? If it is, you can fight for the freedom to think and function at a higher level by replacing yourself. The greatest success stories come when the leader gives up control in a category because it allowed them to be better elsewhere. There are not very many great success stories where it was completely a one-person show. People who have a hard time giving up control either carry that personality trait or have given up control in the past and got stung because of it. You can still maintain a leadership role and oversee the operation while holding others accountable. With all of that power, are you really giving up control?

Ultimately, you are creating a network or system that is comparable to a gravitational pull, because you are perpetuating energy, sharing, creating more resources, and different forms of efficiencies. Just as nature evolves for survival, vision advances to a better state of stabilization and re-creation. It does not happen overnight. When you go through Strategic Visionary

Planning, you are subliminally, almost intentionally, creating a force to facilitate expansion and acceleration. With this energy, you are now stringing together the elements you chose to replace yourself and move forward. Every great replacement, every great delegation, every great leader created means more ideas, more resources, and more time. Think of all the things you can create with more resources, energy, and time. While you are replacing yourself expansion and acceleration are occurring because the person whom replaces you has new ideas and another 24-hour day. Think of all the things that you can create with an extra day.

This stage creates amazing stability. The value of each replacement and each department becomes more productive and more prepared for future steps. Whether it is an intellectual value or a capital value, it is now worth more. It is the ultimate way to accelerate and expand. You can get more financial capital, more collaboration and more freedom to expand your mind. Replacing yourself is a by-product of success indicating that your system is self-sustaining. Now the energy that is in your system willfully expands and accelerates under what you've created. Meanwhile, you are free to create a new entity that will also expand and accelerate. The number of times that can be done, in my opinion, is infinite. Replacing yourself should start today.

CONCLUSION

Thank you for seeking to strengthen your existence through the insights of this book. It is a tribute to your desire for self-improvement and to play a role in the events of your life and beyond. You will be rewarded by arranging creation's energy to achieve the positive results of your vision. Your visionary integrity will align forces to provide opportunity to abundantly supply the joys of life.

The unlimited benefits that you unfold will appear solidly as objects in your life. Then there will be the continuation of a blessing that you sparked. Now you can begin this helpful process granted by God, whose glory will be magnified through you. **Vision is your pathway to victory.**

ABOUT THE AUTHOR

Gordon D'Angelo is co-founder and Chairman of NEXT Financial Group, Inc., the seven-time Broker/Dealer of the Year Award winner, and Chairman and CEO of NEXT Financial Holdings, Inc., handling over 16 billion dollars in assets.

Gordon was an original founder and director of Jackson Hewitt Tax Service. He has consulted for two of the top fifteen franchises in the world, and has founded numerous successful companies. He currently sits on the Board of Directors at Liberty Tax Service.

He appeared for 10 years on Virginia radio show, Ask the Expert, and has been a guest on every major network affiliate, including ABC, CBS, FOX and NBC. Gordon has spoken to many financial, private, and charitable organizations nationally. His easy to grasp Strategic Visionary Planning has been instrumental to companies and individuals seeking stronger creative energy and output.

He makes himself available to those organizations that seek top line performance. Recipients of his engagements have not only sensed, but caught his entrepreneurial spirit making life changing differences. Gordon's passion is to take *Vision: Your Pathway to Victory* and its meaning worldwide, invigorating all participants.

*Based on a poll of registered representatives conducted by Investment Advisor Magazine. Broker/Dealers rated highest by their representatives are awarded "Broker/Dealer of the Year"

APPENDIX

The following tools and templates were designed specifically for Strategic Visionary Planning to help organize and exemplify your unstoppable vision.

My Wish List

1. _____

2. _____

3. _____

4. _____

5. _____

6. _____

7. _____

8. _____

9. _____

10. _____

11. _____

12. _____

13. _____

14. _____

15. _____

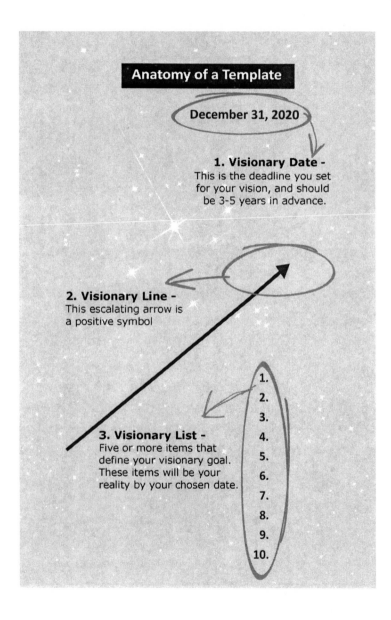

Anatomy of a Template

December 31, 2020

1. Visionary Date -
This is the deadline you set
for your vision, and should
be 3-5 years in advance.

2. Visionary Line -
This escalating arrow is
a positive symbol

3. Visionary List -
Five or more items that
define your visionary goal.
These items will be your
reality by your chosen date.

1.
2.
3.
4.
5.
6.
7.
8.
9.
10.

Your Visionary Template

Date:_____

Name:_____

1.
2.
3.
4.
5.
6.
7.
8.
9.
10.

Bridge Numbers

Year 3

Year 2

Year 1

Year 1
1.
2.
3.
4.
5.
6.
7.
8.
9.
10.

Year 2
1.
2.
3.
4.
5.
6.
7.
8.
9.
10.

Year 3
1.
2.
3.
4.
5.
6.
7.
8.
9.
10.

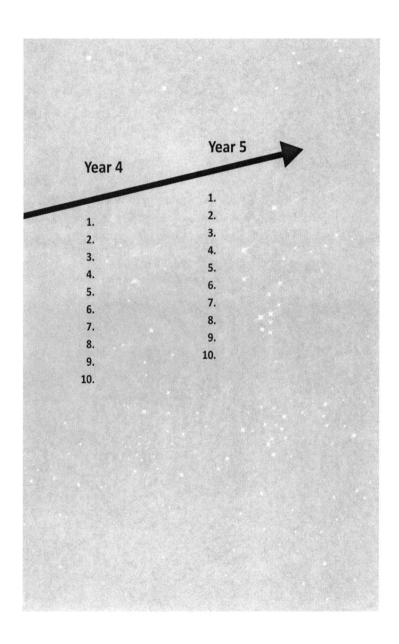

Year 5

Year 4

1.
2.
3.
4.
5.
6.
7.
8.
9.
10.

1.
2.
3.
4.
5.
6.
7.
8.
9.
10.

Initiatives

Year 3

Year 2

Year 1

Year 1

1.
2.
3.
4.
5.
6.
7.
8.
9.
10.

Year 2

1.
2.
3.
4.
5.
6.
7.
8.
9.
10.

Year 3

1.
2.
3.
4.
5.
6.
7.
8.
9.
10.

Date:_____

Name:_____

Year 5

Year 4

1.
2.
3.
4.
5.
6.
7.
8.
9.
10.

1.
2.
3.
4.
5.
6.
7.
8.
9.
10.

Key Players List

1. _____

2. _____

3. _____

4. _____

5. _____

6. _____

7. _____

8. _____

9. _____

10. _____

11. _____

12. _____

13. _____

14. _____

15. _____

Start the Starters List

Name	Functions and Success
1. _____	_____
2. _____	_____
3. _____	_____
4. _____	_____
5. _____	_____
6. _____	_____
7. _____	_____
8. _____	_____
9. _____	_____
10. _____	_____

Helping People

Who Can I Help?	How Can I Help?
1.	
2.	
3.	
4.	
5.	
6.	
7.	
8.	
9.	
10.	

People Helping

Who Can Help Me?	How Can They Help Me?
1.	
2.	
3.	
4.	
5.	
6.	
7.	
8.	
9.	
10.	

Zee IVANOVA

CPSIA information can be obtained at www.ICGtesting.com
Printed in the USA
LVOW062054200612

286956LV00001B/4/P